turning
the hearts of the
fathers

CHRISTIAN LEADERS SPEAK OUT ON REACHING A NEW GENERATION

turning
the hearts of the fathers

CHRISTIAN LEADERS SPEAK OUT ON REACHING A NEW GENERATION

contributing
writers

tommy barnett

ed cole

ted haggard

jack hayford

ron luce

joyce meyer

myles munroe

luis palau

david shibley

jay strack

compiled by
ron luce

ALBURY PUBLISHING
Tulsa, Oklahoma

Turning the Hearts of the Fathers
Christian Leaders Speak Out on Reaching a New Generation
ISBN 1-57778-113-9
Copyright © 1999 by Ron Luce
P. O. Box 2000
Garden Valley, Texas 75771-2000

Published by ALBURY PUBLISHING
P. O. Box 470406
Tulsa, Oklahoma 74147-0406

contents

introduction

by ron luce

Do you know there's an invasion about to happen? This invasion is not from China or Russia. This invasion is coming from within. We're about to be invaded by *teenagers* — children of the baby boomers. Over the next seven to eight years, we're going to see an increase from about twenty-four million present teenagers to thirty-five million. In fact, the next huge population surge in America will happen over these next ten years. That means over sixty million young people between the ages right now of five and eighteen will come through the ranks and take their place in American society as tomorrow's leaders. (Ellen Neuborne et al., "Generation Y," *Business Week* (February 15, 1999): p. 82)

What are the implications of this invasion? What does it mean for us as pastors, parents, and leaders? Think about it for a minute. If the same percentage of young people still get pregnant out of wedlock, there will be a lot more unwed mothers. If the percentage of young people involved in drug abuse stays the same, there will be a lot more young people on drugs. According to the 1999 Drug Control Strategy Report from the White House, illicit drug use among 8th graders more than doubled from 5.7 percent to 14.6 percent. Drug use among 10th graders also doubled in the same period, from 11.6 percent to 23.2 percent. Illicit drug use among 12th graders increased by 50 percent, from 16.4 percent to 24.6 percent. In 1997, 11.4 percent of those aged twelve to seventeen were current drug users, where it was only at 5.3 percent in 1992. If the percentage of youth-related shootings stays the same, there will be a lot more young people hurting and killing others. We're also going to have to build a lot more junior and senior high schools in order to accommodate these young people. We're going to have to do a lot more of everything.

This invasion that's beginning to take place has not gone unnoticed by the world. Madison Avenue and Hollywood are among those gearing up for this young generation. They're already targeting this age group to market their chips, shoes, clothes, facial products, hair products, and sports products, because they know if they get them buying while they're young, they'll buy for the rest of their lives. They are out to win their market share.

We've heard recent revelations about Joe Camel and other cigarette companies targeting thirteen-year-olds, because that's virtually the only place they can get new customers — nonsmoking young people. You can look at just about any commercial on television in the afternoons and evenings and see the advertising is directed towards young people — no matter what the product is. They are targeting our young people.

The real tragedy is that the people selling clothing, cigarettes, movies, and music are targeting young people for their money, but are also getting their hearts. The industry goes after the initial buck and ends up transforming the way young people think, the way they live, and the way they believe. MTV is so aggressive in their determination to go after this young generation. They boast not that they advertise to this generation, but that they "own" this generation. If the world is this aggressive about going after our young people, can't we as the body of Christ be even more aggressive? Yes! Not only can we be more aggressive, it is our *responsibility* to win our young people for the Lord!

Statistics show that over 80 percent of anyone who ever gives their heart to Jesus does so before they're twenty years old. What does that say to you about the importance of reaching this young generation? The highest probability that they'll ever give their life to the Lord is while they're young — before they turn twenty, and get hard and set in their ways. The world knows this and that's why they concentrate on selling them their products while they're young. The same is true with the things of God. If they don't grab hold of the Lord while they're young, chances are they'll get set in their ways, they'll never give their life to the Lord, and they'll never see heaven. I admonish you to seize the opportunity at hand.

The pages that are about to unfold before you will give you insight as to what this generation is thinking, feeling, and seeing. In addition, you'll get a clear picture of what you as a parent, as a pastor, as a leader, as a friend, or as a grandparent can do and must do to reach out and rescue this generation.

It's time for us to realize that the job of reaching this generation is not the youth pastor's job or the youth evangelist's job. It's not even the pastor's job. If you're a Christian and you love the Lord, it's your job — it's all of our jobs. Think of the combined forces of the thousands of people who work in the entertainment industry — Hollywood, MTV, and the music business — all gearing towards grabbing the hearts and dollars of our young people. Yet as Christians, many times all we do is hire one person — an underpaid, inferior, "staff position" — to be our Christian representative in an effort to reach these young people.

Could it be that the world is more committed to reaching out and capturing this generation than we are? Whatever this generation says, believes, and does will shape the next one hundred years both here in America and around the world. Right now is our chance of a lifetime to set the pace for the new millennium by capturing this generation's hearts and winning them to the Lord.

As you read through these pages, realize that this is not just another generation and you're not just another adult watching life go by. God brought you to this world for such a time as this, just like Esther, that you could be a part of shaping a young generation and in so doing, shaping the destiny of a new millennium. God bless you as you find your role in shaping this generation.

UNDERSTANDING THIS GENERATION

chapter one

It's our responsibility as parents and leaders to have the spirit and the attitude of Boaz. He saw a need, and with the same attitude as Christ did later for all of us, reached out to minister to Ruth. (See Ruth 3,4.) Today, we have a generation that's hurting and broken like Ruth. It's been torn apart by their families, destroyed by society, and pillaged by values crammed down their throat. Just like Boaz, we must first acknowledge that there's pain all around us. Secondly, we must pay the price. What is the price? It is whatever it takes to reach out and touch our young people's lives. Thirdly, we must bring them to full recovery. It's time for us to quit walking by saying, "Isn't that too bad and isn't it a shame that all those bad things are happening to these young people? What can I possibly do?" Begin to ask the Lord right now to fill your heart with compassion for a generation of young people all around you who are hurting. Ask Him to give you someone right now who you can begin to pay the price for and bring them to full recovery.

ron

more than a savior

by jack hayford

Filled with drama and emotion, the book of Ruth tells the story of a young woman who lost everything but her will to trust in God. It concludes with her marriage to a man named Boaz, whose principal role in Ruth's life is defined in a single word: *redeemer.* (See Ruth 4:4-10.)

The purpose of this piece of history being included in the Bible may have been to describe the entrance of a Gentile woman into the ancestral bloodline of the Messiah, but students of the Bible see an even grander lesson. Here is great insight into God's way of dealing with ruined people. Here is the picture of the "kinsman-redeemer" — a role and a relationship God gave under the old covenant in order to help us understand His ways under the new covenant.

The kinsman-redeemer law stated that if someone lost his possessions through the death of a loved one, another of his kin could volunteer to repossess that which was lost. (See Leviticus 25:24,25.) The kinsman's redeemer role was fulfilled in two ways: 1) he had to acknowledge his relationship with the one who had suffered loss; and 2) he had to pay the required price for the recovery of what had been lost.

Boaz became both rescuer and restorer. Ruth was a foreigner and an alien in a new cultural environment. Boaz received the disenfranchised widow as his wife and graciously secured her future through restoration of property she otherwise would have lost.

The power of this story transcends its immediate beauty, emotion, and historical significance. Its force emerges in its dynamic picture of what Jesus Christ has done and will do for everyone who puts their trust in Him. Jesus is our Savior, but He is even more than that! He is more than a forgiver of our sins. He is even more than our provider of eternal life. He is our Redeemer! He is the One who is ready to recover and restore what the power of sin and death has taken from us.

It is a mighty truth and worthy of our deepest understanding. Here's how He does it.

he acknowledges us

The kinsman-redeemer pictured in the Old Testament had to step forward in open declaration of his relationship to the individual who had been shamed, embarrassed, or ruined by loss or failure. Just as Boaz responded to Ruth's appeal for help, the Lord Jesus Christ has fully come to us as a Kinsman. **The Word became flesh and made his dwelling among us** (John 1:14 NIV). God became "kin" to mankind! He took upon Himself the form of a servant and was made in the likeness of men. (See Philippians 2:7.) He fully demonstrated His willingness to associate with us, even though we have sinned against Him. He who never sinned at all was willing to be invested with our sin in order to become our Sin-Bearer and Savior. (See 2 Corinthians 5:21.)

Having become one of us, He went one step further. He personally acknowledges a relationship with each of us: "He is not ashamed to call each of us His brothers, His sisters, His very own family" (Hebrews 2:11, author's paraphrase). No matter how badly we have failed, and no matter how far we have fallen, we are not beyond His reach, nor will our sins prevent Him from willingly identifying with us. He has become our Kinsman, and He is ready to claim association with any who will come to Him.

he paid the price

The word *redeem,* as used in the Bible, describes a price that has been paid. In the pawn shop usage of the term, a broker gives a "redemption ticket" that a person may use to reclaim something he has sold for far less than it's worth. This pawn shop image holds a powerful lesson and provides a dramatic picture of the way sin works in human lives — tempting us to sell out for less than God's promised blessing, and leaving us with little or nothing as a reward. Yet, as with the rules of the pawn shop redemption, recovery occurs when a greater price is paid for redeeming that which has been sold cheap and lost. That is what Jesus did as Savior.

In him we have redemption through his blood, the forgiveness of sins, in accordance with the riches of God's grace.

Ephesians 1:7 NIV

Forasmuch as ye know that ye were not redeemed with corruptible things, as silver and gold, from your vain conversation received by tradition from your fathers;
But with the precious blood of Christ, as a lamb without blemish and without spot.

1 Peter 1:18,19

Everything Jesus offers of new life, new hope, and new possibilities is guaranteed to us on the basis of a total and complete payment.

he brings full recovery

Few realize the thrilling truth that Christ's payment for our redemption involves an ongoing, continual process of *recovery.* The significance of that provision is clearly apparent when we assess the destructive impact of sin and failure on the human personality.

How many have suffered loss because of sin? So many have been injured, broken, and damaged. People are too often left with emotional, physical, and mental casualties as a result of human failure. The failure may not even be one's own. Damage can often be the result of someone else's neglect, exploitation, or violation. On the other hand, the loss may be the individual's own just due, resulting from conscious rebellion or defiance toward what they knew to be right. Nevertheless, the wreckage wrought in any of our lives may be mended as surely as the sin may be forgiven.

The precious truth of Jesus' power as Redeemer is that He has a plan and an ability to progressively restore the broken parts of human experience and to reproduce a whole person. His salvation is not only an act of forgiveness, it is also a progressive action of redemption. He not only meets us at the moment of our new birth, but His saving life generates a momentum which can bring us into the fullness of restored life and joy.

jack hayford

The precious truth
of Jesus' power as
Redeemer is that
He has a plan and
an ability to
progressively restore
the broken parts
of human experience
and to reproduce
a whole person.

I believe there is no dearer truth in the Word of God than this: **He is able also to save them to the uttermost that come unto God by him** (Hebrews 7:25). That simply means that in the recovery process, there is no distance too great for Him to restore us.

God said to the farmers of ancient Israel, **I will restore to you the years that the locust hath eaten** (Joel 2:25). In those words, He gave us a promise answering our present need as well. Whatever has been decayed or destroyed, He is our Restorer, Recoverer, and Redeemer!

Whatever your loss, pain, failure, or brokenness, Jesus Christ is fully capable of bringing about change unto full restoration. Just as His resurrection power brings new life, His redemption power brings new hope. He is able, for He's more than a Savior — He's your Redeemer who promises He will give **beauty for ashes, the oil of joy for mourning** (Isaiah 61:3).

Just as you gave Him your heart and received Him as Savior, give Him your life's broken pieces. Receive Him as Redeemer. Give Him time to work a full redemptive recovery in each part of your life. Let these promises be set in motion as, in childlike faith, you receive His commitment to restore everything sin has damaged, lost, or ruined.

Begin now to praise Him! You will discover that worshipping Him is the light that leads you out of the darkness and out of all the despair over sin's effect and aftermath. Let God's redemptive power and life flow as you praise Jesus Christ — your Savior and your Redeemer!

chapter two

What you're about to read is a heartwarming account of a pastor's heart towards young people. It's an account of a father passing on a heritage to his sons and the sons' reflections on how their father influenced their lives. This is an excellent example of what this generation needs — someone who cares enough to impact every young person around them. It's up to us to pass on a heritage to our own children, both those in our home and those who surround us. It's up to us to pass on a heritage to the sons and daughters of America — those we find in our neighborhood, those without fathers, those without mothers, those without Christian parents, and those who have no one they can look up to, honor, and respect.

As Christian leaders, we should be the ones they can look up to. We should be investing our hearts and lives into this generation. We need to wrap our arms around them and be willing to say, "If no one else chooses to father you, we'll father you, we'll parent you, and we'll encourage you." It's not only our right to do so, it's our responsibility.

For every testimony like Luke's and Matthew's, which you are about to read, there are hundreds of others in America who have no father or mother they can look up to — no one who accepts and loves them unconditionally. Look around you for opportunities to create a testimony like these. With your involvement, their lives can be changed.

ron

fathering this generation

by tommy barnett

Often during the years when my sons were young, we would shoot baskets at our favorite hoop. No matter the weariness of my church schedule or packed agenda for the next day, it was nothing short of this father's joy to carve out time to spend with his kids. Even as the boys' skills grew and they scored more slam-dunks than their dad, those experiences were a bonding process and oxygen for my soul! Years later, with both sons grown, I have driven by that spot and thanked God for the times we dribbled balls and defined strategies on a neighborhood basketball court. Our *esprit de corps* developed early, because I made a firm commitment to my family.

In Genesis 12, Abraham built an altar to God. In Genesis 26, his son Isaac did the same. Those opening chapters of the Bible relate a strong message to fathers. For good or bad, the phrase is commonly used, "Like father, like son." It is no surprise that example is not just one thing, it is *everything*. How do I know? My dad, Herschel Barnett, was pastor of a great church in Kansas City, and I observed his love for the people and unrelenting example of winning souls to Jesus Christ. I wanted to be just like him.

Abraham could have told Isaac the benefits of worship and sent him elsewhere to receive instruction, but instead, he set the example. As we're nearing the end of the twentieth century, I challenge fathers and leaders to model themselves after Jesus Christ. My church is aware that they only follow me as I follow Christ.

The question becomes increasingly relevant: *Why is Christian faith not self-propagating?* If God ordained the physical family to be "fruitful and multiply," surely He has ordained the Christian family to do the same. (See Genesis 1:28.) The intentions of God are that **one generation shall praise thy works to another, and shall declare thy mighty acts…My mouth shall speak the praise of the Lord: and let all flesh bless his holy name for ever and ever** (Psalm 145:4,21).

Why, then, have so many sons vanished into the landscape of mediocrity and placed building the kingdom of God of lessor importance? My heart cries out when I witness the current trend of optional morality and descending integrity. I see a declining respect and awe of Father God. It is up to us as pastors and leaders to reverse the trend. America is in a crisis. The changes may be subtle, but they are sure. One only has to study history to be reunited with the rise and fall of civilizations. The normalization of evil is acceptable to many in the disconnected society. So how does this impact the Church? It already has, as we have been forcefully confronted with the knowledge that countless of the last few generations have strayed from their Christian heritage.

A talk show host recently asked his guest if America was just another piece of real estate, no different from other countries of the world, and if so, will it fall off the face of history from the fast decline? The guest could not give a positive answer. Therein lies our mandate. If the foundations fall, what are the righteous to do? They are to continue in righteousness.

> **Righteousness exalts a nation, but sin is a disgrace to any people.**
> **Proverbs 14:34 NASB**

Our further summons, in spite of pessimists, comes from Jesus, "My Father works unceasingly, and so do I." (John 5:17 WEY, KREG)

The generations that preceded us did just that. They gave God their best and passed the baton. Their sacrifices of service for Jesus Christ were more than a "reasonable" service. (See Romans 12:1.) God was an integral part of their lives. Faithfulness and godly example are pillars in established families. Bringing up children in the Lord means more than occasional trips to church or Sunday school. Giving beyond their limits was the norm of those in my past. Dare I do less?

When I committed my life to the Lord, barely in my teens, no bells or whistles went off in Dad's church. In the past, when great athletes or known people made a decision to follow Jesus, there was great excitement on what the individuals could do for Jesus. When I presented my small frame of eighty pounds at the altar, I wonder what the congregation perceived. In retrospect, their perception wasn't important. The Spirit of

God knew I gave everything at that altar. I knew I wanted to preach. My career was spent in evangelism, but innately, I believed I would pastor. Crusading is important, but conserving the flock and multiplying for the glory of God was my heart's desire.

In the New Testament church, people were added daily. (See Acts 2:47.) That is quite a feat. But it never discouraged me, because I had watched my dad, and he made indelible impressions on me on the greatness of God. He preached on street corners, held meetings on the courthouse steps, moved from schoolhouse to schoolhouse, and never overlooked those disenfranchised. His church grew in numbers and outreach. Every Sunday, he packed his automobile with people who had no other transportation, and until the day he joined heaven, he never let up. He acknowledged that his heavenly Father worked unceasingly, and so must he.

At ten years of age, wanting to be like Dad, I preached to the trees in a city park and used the old stumps for a pulpit. At other times, I would solicit my buddies to be the congregation, load them onto one of Dad's parked buses, and from the driver's seat, I shared the Lord.

My implicit trust in God grew when, as a sixteen-year-old, my uncle invited my dad to speak at his church. It was not possible for him to accept the invitation, but Dad said he would send me. After all, I was becoming a chip off the old block! Uncle responded that he didn't want the chip, he wanted the block. They got the chip!

I preached one of Dad's sermons the first night and two couples came to Christ. No words could express the elation and humility to God for using me. That night, I couldn't sleep as I envisioned multitudes of men, women, and children coming down the aisle to receive Jesus as Savior and Lord. The second night, as I focused on the faces of those two couples, I prayed God would give me forty-six more souls and then I would know I was really called to preach.

My uncle was concerned with my apparent "numbers fleece." He reminded me that the city I was in, Seminole, Texas, was a small town and rarely did the church have seventy in Sunday school. I was not daunted. As the revival continued the people grew in number. I was so new at preaching that I had to repeat Dad's sermons! However, on the last night, four men and two women were the first to come down to the front. Soon others joined them. I counted in almost disbelief — forty-five…forty-six…forty-seven…forty-eight…forty-nine…FIFTY!

My uncle and I were up most of the night rejoicing. We were so exhilarated. And then it crossed my heart, *What if I had asked for one hundred souls?* Doesn't the Bible say, **according to your faith be it unto you** (Matthew 9:29)? Suddenly, it was quiet around that kitchen table. Again, I saw those same multitudes I had seen before and I observed people who were just "waiting to be asked." So began my personal portrait of the vision of people being added to church daily.

God has been more than gracious to me. He has blessed me with a magnificent wife and three children. I often prayed that if God tarried, my children would pick up the baton that had been passed down throughout the generations in my heritage. Those prayers were heard and my sons have become the fifth generation to serve the Lord. Now I pray it will pass to their sons and daughters. Multitudes have a great need for the Lord and the Lord has a great need for the multitudes.

The process of my sons, Luke and Matthew, serving God in a full-time capacity was not always obvious. I also knew that God calls most into secular work, though I am hard pressed to separate the sacred and secular. We all are to be His witnesses in whatever endeavor chosen.

I wanted each son to relate his personal experience, which may not be unlike other youth reading this chapter. My oldest, Luke, relates:

"I grew up having a lot of fun with my dad. He always came home for dinner and we would be together as a family before he usually returned to church. As a boy, I watched him virtually every Sunday run to the door to greet the people. He made a point to love and welcome everyone. For a time, I wondered why he did that. The people respected him from the pulpit, but I soon observed that his individual words to each one were genuine and from his heart. The only explanation as I matured was his endless pursuit of reaching people. He was building up their faith in his sermons and affirming their importance as individuals at the door.

"His example influenced my heart. In my adolescent years, I had no desire to be in ministry. I had seen Dad's heartaches, pains, trials, and tribulations, and wanted no part of that kind of church treatment. I pursued a career in professional golf and was satisfied in making a lot of money and performing on national television. Was that a great calling? As always, Mom and Dad were supportive and encouraged me to be my best. I was never pushed toward ministry, but so often Dad's voice resonated as he would share that 'a minister walks a road of trials and tribulations, but along with the difficulties comes the great joy of seeing people's lives changed by the power of the Holy God.' I also recall his admonition of never going into the ministry until you're confident you've been called of God.

"The day came when Dad suggested that if ever an opportunity arose and I was asked to speak at a church, I should accept. He was not being controlling, it was a quiet suggestion. I felt safe in agreeing, because no established church was going to offer an uninterested, unmotivated, apathetic preacher's son a speaking engagement. I had never even led a public prayer in a worship service. I just didn't think it would happen — but it did!

"What a shock! Just as I was feeling safe in my career choice, God had a way of stirring me up and pulling me out of my comfort zone. About two weeks after our discussion, a pastor in Arizona called and requested that I speak at his church. I ran to Dad's office, knowing it was a "setup." His response was one of surprise, as he had no idea what I was talking about. He did remind me of our prior conversation and that I had said I would accept an invitation if offered.

"Suddenly, God had invaded my twenty-two-year-old life and was allowing me a divine option. Option or mandate, I was unsure. I begged Dad to get me out of the invitation, because I was painfully aware I would fold right in front of the audience.

"I had been taught in precept and example to keep my word. I prepared as best I could, and when the time came, I nervously walked to the podium. I delivered a somewhat confused message. However, one thing I did know was how to give an invitation. Dad never passed up a chance and I believed it was part of what every pastor did. I asked anyone who wanted to give their life to the Lord to come to the front, fully convinced no one would. And then I saw a lady with tears streaming down her face. She accepted the Lord.

"As tears welled up in my eyes, I had a fearful thought. *If I had not heeded the call to speak in that church, would that precious lady have spent eternity without Jesus?* My career began to change that day by the grace and call of God.

"I started, like Dad, as an evangelist. I preached wherever I was asked and prayed and prepared as if my life depended on it. It did! My confidence is in God, because faithful is He who called you who will also do it. (See Romans 4:21.)

"Dad is my hero. I learn from him constantly that this is *the hour* to reach the lost. Time may be running out. His sincerity and authenticity are the models I follow, and I have received much revelation and motivation from him.

"Has it been easy? Never! The journey to the church I now pastor was not smooth. I have experienced off-ramps and detours I never anticipated, but God led my wife and me to Beaver Creek First Assembly. We started with about two hundred dear people. We met in schools, a Holiday Inn, and then took the step of purchasing property. The structure held 1,700 and needed refurbishing. What a challenge. Impossible? **With God all things are possible** (Matthew 19:26). Our growth is great. We have purchased four buses and a wheelchair bus, and we anticipate 2,000 members by the year 2000!

"Dad's example of Christ's admonition that **the Lord added to the church daily** (Acts 2:47) is my mandate too. When traveling to speak in another church, I'm often greeted at an airport by someone who transported Dad in the past. The odds are high they will relate similar stories. When he visits a church or convocation, he is one of the few visiting preachers who will remain after the service until the last person leaves — praying, loving, and caring for that group even as he does at his own church, Phoenix First Assembly.

"I encourage young people who, like myself in the past, may have a dream carved out for the future, to give the Holy Spirit an opportunity to speak to you and to be faithful in whatever calling. Never neglect to stir up the gift that is within you. (See 2 Timothy 1:6.) The high calling of ministering to those who may never have been asked to receive Jesus as Savior and Lord is worth living and dying for."

Matthew was called to the ministry in his teens, and his story is different.

"As the son of Tommy Barnett, the people in Dad's church had great expectations for me, but I was the insecure child in our family. I would see Dad and his great success for God and balance that against my timidity and fear.

"I believed in the ministry, because I believed in the integrity of my father. He lived what he preached. We always knew he loved his congregation, but he loved Mom and us kids best of all — second only to God. I knew Dad's character was above reproach and, most of all, he was my good friend. On Sunday, he changed roles and became my pastor. One constant was ever before me — I wanted to be like him, but I knew I would never possess the courage to do what he did every day, seven days a week. So, I kept trying to run from it. He never discussed it with me and he reiterated to his three children that the choice of our future was in God's and our hands.

"The people in our church kept a heavy burden on me. I was often reminded that if I entered the ministry, I would have some big shoes to fill. With so many expectations, I wanted to move out of Dad's shadow. However, as I matured, I listened to the message of his life and to his preaching and God began to deal with me, challenging me when I was thirteen years old. I had watched my dad leave every morning to go to the mountainside of his church to pray and seek God for hours. It was becoming clear that those times alone with God were the source of his power, so I started praying an hour a day or more. I was seeking to get closer to God while asking for an infusion of courage — a big one!

"After church service, I would wait two or three hours just so I could ride home with Dad while my friends had already split or left for pizza. I wanted to ask questions and learn what made him who he is to people. Those moments built great faith in me, because I was seeing that ordinary people can do extraordinary things for God. God and Dad were building confidence in me. Dad praised my athletic ability and encouraged me. He was always available, one-on-one, and shared his pride in his family.

"As I evaluated my developing love for God and people, I felt compelled to take some faltering steps of faith and launch out on my own to see how much my faith and confidence had progressed. I ventured to Mill Avenue by the campus of Arizona State University. While not quite as radical and liberal as Telegraph Avenue at Berkeley, it still had the personality types of sixty thousand students. Picking a street corner with fear and trepidation, I started telling passersby that Jesus loved them. Every Friday night, for the next eight to ten months, I was there by myself until some friends joined my secret mission.

"I became bolder and more self-assured as I shared Jesus all around that corner and walkway. I was also building character in my life and learning so much. Scary? It really was, but God was opening my vision to a reachable, lost world. God was showing me that He was the source of my courage.

Have I not commanded you? Be strong and courageous! Do not tremble or be dismayed, for the Lord your God is with you wherever you go.

Joshua 1:9 NASB

"People carry so much condemnation and discouragement with them, and walk around with so many hell-like situations at their heels, that even the words 'God bless you,' or 'Have a great week and stay out of trouble,' brought a response. For a few minutes on that street corner, I would preach the same message over and over of God's forgiveness and love. People began to stop and listen to the message, and I saw souls born into the kingdom of God.

"On my sixteenth birthday, Dad called and said that our Church on the Street needed someone to preach that night. He wondered if I might be available. I said, "Yes," and realized I was in a bind, for I had never preached like that in a church, let alone the inner city. I was nervous, scattered, and didn't think I would do well. I used a combination of Dad's messages, phrases, and altar calls. The message was simple —

heaven or hell, each must choose a destination! At the end, one man came to the altar crying and weeping. He accepted Jesus and went into the street proclaiming, 'I've been saved.' I witnessed an instant transformation.

"That night, I experienced mixed emotions. It was my birthday and I had been given a precious present with eternal value. I had reached beyond myself and saw the lives of people without Christ as my responsibility. I held another secret within, for one night when sitting on the hood of my car a few months previously, I had asked God what He wanted me to do with my life. I asked Him to show me my destiny. I knew my brother Luke and I were different. I was an idealist who wanted to show people how far they can go with God and then take them to the furthermost point possible. The realist will take those people by the hand and lead them. I kept *seeing* their eternal destiny.

"Sitting under the stars, I also *saw* Los Angeles in my heart. The insecurities were diminishing. I was willing. I knew Dad had great cities on his heart since he was a kid. I believed, though no one had asked, that I would be ministering in Los Angeles by age twenty. All this time, God was instructing me that rather than following in Dad's footsteps, I should be concentrating on following in HIS.

"As a senior in high school, I was preaching thirty-five weeks of the year someplace near and far. I would take a plane, just like Dad did, but in a different direction, sharing with youth and returning in time to go back to school on Monday. After high school, the opportunities increased. When I went to share the Lord, like Dad, I would stay until the last person was gone, shaking everyone's hand, talking with them, and praying with them. When it would end, my mind returned to the night I sat on the hood of the car and *saw* Los Angeles.

"Even during those years, Dad, my brother, and I still shot a lot of baskets or played golf when he was available. He was always peppered with questions about ministry. The chief one in my mind was when there are so many unsaved people in the world, why do most churches appear to cater to Christians? Why doesn't the church speak what relates to the lost, the least, and the lonely? Though Dad would answer, he would always bring us back to the center with his wisdom to keep ministry balanced. We always ended our conversation with a major area of agreement — discussing the need to address the unsaved in new, innovative ways.

"When the time came and God led Dad to Los Angeles, I was offered the job of errand boy, secretary, youth worker, part-time, full-time, all the time — anything I could do to help. It was a joy, because I was in Los Angeles! Dad asked many pastors to come and pastor the fledgling, inner city church we began. He already led a major church, but he never stepped away from a challenge. During the time of planning, praying, and seeking a location, often the enemy of discouragement crept in, but we never lost sight of the vision. Dad always preaches that there is a miracle in every house. When there was no one else to pastor, he looked in our house and considered me as co-pastor with him. My dream became a reality.

"The ministry of the Los Angeles Dream Center has grown and increased. Others are following our plan in cities across the United States. Our network of multiple ministries working together is becoming a template for others. Thousands of individuals have been introduced to Jesus. We now, at the massive former property of the Queen of Angeles Hospital, are a 'hospital' prescribing God's love, meeting needs, healing hurts, and most of all, winning souls."

The future for the Barnetts and each reader is as bright as the kept promise of God! My sons and I still shoot an occasional basket and more often may catch the same plane to share Christ. Our message is much the same. We all need to take another look at the local church. Are we preparing for the future generations? I believe every individual Christian affects eternity. No one truly knows where their influence begins or where it stops. As pastors, parents, and leaders, none of us can see just where the radical changes we witness in today's world will lead us. We do know we must plan for the days ahead. Are we prepared to meet the spiritual challenges or will tomorrow find us out of breath?

I was given a copy of a Gallup survey that interested me. The question asked was, *How close do the American family members feel to each other?* I probably should not have been surprised at the answers, considering the disintegrating family structure. About 90 percent were close to their mothers, 85 percent to sisters and brothers, 75 percent to a grandparent or grandparents, but less than half to their fathers. It made me think of Matthew dreading Father's Day, because in Los Angeles, few of those being reached at the Dream Center have or know a father. A real father's heart has never been turned toward them. They have never had a father who was interested in their homework, would play ball with them, or would listen to their hopes and aspirations. Instead, they look to rock stars rather than the Rock — Jesus Christ. Some seek soothsayers, because no one else has ever asked them about knowing our Savior. Understanding Father God's love takes time to comprehend. There are too few godly individuals who are willing to hold high the cross and make clear what was accomplished at Calvary for every person. **The harvest is plentiful, but the workers are few** (Matthew 9:37 NASB). Very few.

I believe that instead of finding fault with the situation confronting us, we are to diligently search for remedies that are centered in Jesus. Criticizing the circumstances may be easier than changing the conditions. Paul said that our God has given us the ability to do certain things well. (See 1 Peter 4:11.) Since He has, we must do them diligently and well.

I would never have imagined God could use me. I am always humbled by His mercy and goodness. I know my inadequacies, but I also have grabbed on to His complete adequacy. As never before, I want to admonish the Christian world to get busy. We need to plant trees under which we will never sit. A strange statement? Not if you read 1 Chronicles 22:1-5 where we see the story of David's desire to build a house worthy of God. Though he was an old man and knew he would never enter into that House of God, he provided the blueprints and materials for the future generations. He prepared abundantly before his death to pass the baton.

I don't know what the future holds, but I do know this — God loves the local church and He wants it to grow, to be strong, and to impact this world. Many say we are living in a post-Christian era. I believe it is true, but it does not impede our responsibility.

A Cyprian in the third century wrote a friend, "It's a bad world. But I've discovered in the midst of it a quiet and holy people who have learned a great secret. They've discovered joy that is thousands of times better than the pleasures of our sinful life.

tommy barnett

We need to plant trees under which we will never sit. A strange statement? Not if you read 1 Chronicles 22:1-5 where we see the story of David's desire to build a house worthy of God. Though he was an old man and knew he would never enter into that House of God, he provided the blueprints and materials for the future generations. He prepared abundantly before his death to pass the baton.

They're despised and some are persecuted, but they don't care. They're masters of their souls. They've overcome the world. These people are Christians, and after studying them, I've become one of them."

We become a true overcomer by first receiving the Lord as Savior. To the Christian, the Bible says, **You are from God, little children, and have overcome them; because greater is He who is in you than he who is in the world** (1 John 4:4 NASB).

> **And I will pray the Father, and he shall give you another Comforter, that he may abide with you for ever;...**
> **But the Comforter, which is the Holy Ghost, whom the Father will send in my name, he shall teach you all things, and bring all things to your remembrance, whatsoever I have said unto you.**
>
> **John 14:16,26**

The Holy Spirit, or Resident Truth Teacher, is our Comforter and Encourager. If we are not doing what we have been called to do, proclaiming the life-changing message of Jesus Christ, we are discouraging the Encourager, the Holy Spirit. He has promised to lead us, guide us, and prepare us for our God-ordained destiny. We must only ask and faithfully act!

What is your vision and plan as we move into the next century? I say it often and repeat it again, **Where there is no vision, the people perish** (Proverbs 29:18). However, burn it into your heart and soul that "where there are no people, the vision perishes."

I am driven by the mandate, **He who wins souls is wise** (Proverbs 11:30 NIV), and **Those who are wise will shine like the brightness of the heavens, and those who lead many to righteousness, like the stars for ever and ever** (Daniel 12:3 NIV). People are the only asset we can take with us into eternity. God's currency is people!

> **The Lord is not slack concerning his promise, as some men count slackness; but is longsuffering to us-ward, not willing that any should perish, but that all should come to repentance.**
>
> **2 Peter 3:9**

My prayer is that the heart of fathers would be turned to their sons and families, engraving upon them the irrevocable truth of God's Word. Only then will the Great Commission be fulfilled and we will experience the words of Isaiah.

The people that walked in darkness have seen a great light: they that dwell in the land of the shadow of death, upon them hath the light shined.
Thou hast multiplied the nation, and not increased the joy: they joy before thee according to the joy in harvest, and as men rejoice when they divide the spoil.

Isaiah 9:2,3

Every believer has been bequeathed a sacred trust from God to share His message and pass the baton of saving faith from one generation to the next until He comes.

chapter three

For too long, the youth pastor has been looked upon as a second-rate, can't-get-a-real-job, kind of person. God is wanting more than an overgrown, teenage baby-sitting service for our young people. He has entrusted the hearts and lives of an entire generation to these valiant men and women. Their choice of involvement or calling doesn't always get the limelight. They often don't hear much of a thank-you, they receive little appreciation, and their's certainly isn't a job one would choose to get rich.

They do it out of a love for young people. They love the unloved and they reach out to the ones who are overlooked by even their own parents. They pray, they cry, and they stay up late talking to young people, because their hearts have been touched for the lambs. It's time for us to begin to esteem these generals leading a new generation. It is time we learn how to properly treat our youth pastors and esteem them in our churches.

ron

a key element in reaching our youth

by ted haggard

I recently listened to one of the most passionate, life-giving sermons I have heard in a long time. The speaker wasn't anyone you would be familiar with, but after listening to him, I was convinced he could be one of the keynote speakers at any Christian gathering. He was intelligent, resourceful, and challenging. He was humble in tone, confident in purpose, and colorful in manner. His topic was memorable and relevant, and he spoke with such gracious authority that I doubt anyone in the audience left untouched that day. He is my youth pastor.

It is easy to be happy with my youth pastor, or any co-worker for that matter, when their performance is top-notch. When the youth group is swelling and kids are successfully learning how to live in Christ, it is not difficult to think highly of the job my youth pastor is doing. But, as I constantly remind myself, my youth pastor isn't just "any staff member." He holds one of the most important positions in the church, and it's my responsibility to ensure that he has the freedom and confidence he needs to do a fantastic job.

After years of ministry, I am convinced that the youth pastor is one of the most significant co-laborers a successful senior pastor can have. In fact, in a time when our churches are highlighting youth ministry more and more, our relationships with our youth pastors could possibly be the single most productive relationship we have.

highlighting the importance of youth ministry

There are a few basic principles that seem to be consistent in most successful churches. For example, I know it is more important to give to missions than to live in ted haggard

After years of ministry, I am convinced that the youth pastor is one of the most significant co-laborers a successful senior pastor can have. In fact, in a time when our churches are highlighting youth ministry more and more, our relationships with our youth pastors could possibly be the single most productive relationship we have.

extravagance. It is more important to pray for the people of my city than it is to pray that the Denver Broncos win the Super Bowl. And most of all, it is more important to have a *friendship* with my youth pastor than to just consider him as someone on staff.

The youth pastor's job at a church isn't just a position to be filled. We are making a major mistake if we ever think the youth pastor is simply an employee or volunteer who fills a remedial role. Instead, youth pastors can be the Michael Jordans of the church world. If we do our work well by building a strong ministry team, our youth ministers can be the most talented, innovative, creative people we have. Because of their roles, they often work the longest hours, listen to the most people, and plan the events that most dramatically impact people's lives.

Unfortunately, most churches do not see it this way and senior pastors, board members, and church members don't adequately value their youth ministers. As a result, they either recruit the wrong person for the youth ministry role, or they allow the wrong type of volunteer to fill the slot.

The average youth minister in America serves for only nine months. It seems as though many of our senior pastors replace their youth pastors more often than they say, "Amen." The stereotype of youth work is often associated with dilapidated old buses, tight budgets, little or no personal income, leftover space that is an afterthought, and an inconsistent and shaky relationship with the senior pastor. It is rare to find a youth pastor who has been in his position for more than three years, and it is even rarer to find a youth group that is steadily growing year after year.

So what's the problem? Are there no good youth ministers? Is a successful youth ministry an impossible feat? Is this just the nature of youth ministry and something we in the church simply must accept?

No. No. And no. The fact is, there are some outstanding youth pastors out there (four of them work for me). But too often, they allow the wrong attitudes or inferior modeling into their spirits and find themselves giving up and leaving their youth ministry roles. Because of dissatisfaction with the structure of their churches, poor interpersonal relationships, or a need to become a senior pastor in order to make the money necessary to sustain their families, high quality youth ministers often resign prematurely, sending a very negative message and hurting the local church. But it doesn't have to happen to us. None of these events have to take place, and none of the resulting negative stereotypes surrounding youth ministries have to be reinforced by any of our churches.

So what is the answer to the problem of youth ministry? Since this chapter is directed toward senior pastors instead of youth ministers, I'll answer the question this way: *We senior pastors need to do our jobs better.*

ask not what your youth pastor can do for you; ask what you can do for your youth pastor!

When I was a youth pastor for Roy Stockstill at Bethany World Prayer Center in Baker, Louisiana, my dad, who lived in Indiana, suffered a heart attack. My mother called and told me that Dad was in the hospital, but his condition was not serious and not to worry. Mom encouraged me to stay in Louisiana and come home for Christmas to see everyone. By then, Daddy would be recovered.

After talking with Mom, I called Brother Roy and told him about Mom's phone call and about Dad's condition. He asked me to come over to his house. When I arrived, he prayed with me for Dad, gave me more than enough money, and told me to go home the next morning to see him. I left on the next plane to find Dad recovering nicely in the hospital. We talked, prayed, and laughed together. A senior pastor who demonstrated his love for me in a tangible way made that time with my dad possible. As I left his hospital room, both of us were smiling and I waved back to him saying that I would see him at Christmas. It never happened. Dad died two weeks later.

After that experience, I knew Brother Roy would protect me and keep me safe. I knew he loved me, which made me want to serve him faithfully and do everything within my strength to strengthen his ministry, his vision, and his calling. I didn't need my own calling. My calling was to serve his calling. I was his youth pastor. So with those decisions, I would do whatever was necessary to be trustworthy, honorable, and faithful to him.

I certainly don't know everything Brother Roy was feeling and thinking during those years, but I do know he trusted me, believed in me, and loved me. I know I tested each of those decisions on his part, but he persevered. He gave me the freedom to do my job with passion. As I did the things that concerned him, and made mistakes that created some problems around the church, he would kindly coach me and cover for me. Even though he was thirty-seven years older than I was, he was a faithful friend in the truest sense. He didn't micro-manage me and he wasn't overly familiar with me, but he did strengthen me. Because of Brother Roy's investment in me, both as an employee and as a friend, I was free to serve.

My experience with Brother Roy taught me that one of the keys to effective youth ministry is to invest in your youth pastor. My wife, Gayle, and I have taken a very specific approach to the way we select and relate to our youth pastor, and it has made all the difference in the world — both in ministry and in our personal lives.

investing in our youth departments

As I mentioned earlier, part of the stereotype of youth work is that they get the worst of what's available — the smallest rooms, the cheapest vans, and the least amount of money. I regularly hear of youth ministers having to work with horrible old buses local schools have auctioned off. I know most churches do the best they can, and certainly youth workers need to be grateful for anything the church can provide, but it's worth it for the church to value the youth ministry enough to give it the best it can provide. Too many church buses are in such bad shape that it is a miracle we don't end up with more young people getting killed.

I learned my lesson. Now that we realize how important youth ministry is, we give the youth department a priority position in the budget with church vehicles and with public exposure. People in our community know that when they become involved with our church, their young people will be ministered to. It is one of our top priorities to insure that their work with their own children will be supplemented with competent youth ministry teams.

There is a trap we need to be aware of. Too often, youth pastors promise a stronger, better ministry if only they could have more staff and/or more money. We senior pastors often say the same thing, but it's not true. Genuine ministry doesn't need additional staff or money. Genuine ministry happens because of a contrite heart before God in the person with the correct gift in the correct position. That's really all it takes. The right person with the right gifts in the right position can be successful. As they are successful with what they have, we as senior pastors should do everything within our power to insure that they have additional staff and funds as their ministry develops.

This principle is important, especially for smaller churches with tight budgets. In small churches, where meeting rooms are hard to come by and things like buses and sound equipment are out of the question, it is imperative to make sure that the congregation is in full support of the youth pastor. If the congregation is behind the youth, there will be a constant flow of vans to borrow, condos to stay in, and houses available for weekly meetings.

I know of one local church in Colorado where the youth department couldn't afford to rent a campground for their annual summer camp. The church knew of the situation, cared about their youth, and was trying to help find a solution. One of the church men, who was a plumber by trade, did a job for a nearby retreat center, and as part of his payment, he asked the retreat center to offer the youth group a greatly discounted rate on their facilities. They consented, and the whole church celebrated as the youth got to go to summer camp.

Stories like this make me smile, because I know that church has simply inherited the senior pastor's love of ministry to young people. This can happen at every church. The amount of money doesn't matter; what matters is a sincere desire to love and support the youth ministries, and a valiant effort to invest in them at every opportunity.

a relationship built on trust

There is no single factor in the senior pastor/youth pastor relationship that is as important as trust. Without trust, you will never be content to give your youth pastor the freedom they need to do a good job. Without trust, you will never have peace (particularly when the youth group is away at camp or on a missions trip). Without trust, your youth pastor will never be able to let their guard down around you. And, most importantly, without trust, your youth pastor will never want to be your friend.

My youth pastor, John Bolin, and I have a simple system regarding the amount of trust I put in him: I trust him 100 percent, and he works with integrity and never breaches that trust. It is as easy as that. Of course, implicit trust must be built over time, but it can never be built unless the senior pastor takes the risk of believing in his youth pastor in the first place.

One of the things I enjoy doing during Sunday morning services is getting up in the pulpit and bragging on our youth department. I don't lie, which means I don't brag unless there is something to brag about. But when a ministry team in the church, including the youth ministry team, is doing a good job, I'll freely and gladly let everyone know.

"Hey, I just want everyone to know what a fantastic job the youth department is doing," I'll say, and then I'll mention something about their upcoming events and how they are growing in the Lord. Not only does this communicate to the church that the youth department is highly prized, but it also reminds John how much I believe in what he is doing.

Privately, John and I talk frankly about the job he is doing. If he is discouraged in any way, we discuss it. If he is bored with his job, we talk about it. If he is excited and feels like God is taking the youth program in a new direction, we dig through the idea together. The secret here is that these conversations are not just business, they are rooted in our friendship, and neither of us are threatened by the fact that we are discussing "work" or that we are in a boss/subordinate relationship.

I have a real relationship with John, not just a corporate one. We are friends and he knows he has the freedom to discuss his job openly. John knows he could come into my office and say, "Ted, I am frustrated, I hate being a youth pastor, and I want to go to law school," and I wouldn't blow up. We would sit down as friends, talk about it, and deal with any problems. In order for him to stay and be happy, he's got to know that he always has the freedom to leave. But if John and I didn't trust each other and didn't work together as friends, none of this would ever be possible.

uprooting the second-class citizen mentality

A youth pastor from Wisconsin (I'll call him "Mark") told me the following story:

Mark was serving in a large church that provided a parsonage for every pastoral staff member. Because the church was growing, a housing shortage developed and the pastors of the church met to discuss the problem. At one point in the meeting, the senior pastor glanced at Mark and got an idea. "Hey, I know," the senior pastor said, "why don't we just have Mark and his family move into the apartment above the youth chapel?"

The "apartment" was a tiny, one-bedroom place over the youth building. Mark's heart sank as he thought of moving his wife and two young children into the apartment. In that moment, Mark lost all confidence in his relationship with his senior pastor. Because he didn't feel like the two of them were friends, he never spoke with the senior pastor about the comment. In the senior pastor's effort to solve a problem, he inadvertently communicated to Mark that his family was not important, and within a few months Mark was "called" to a position in another church.

John has told me that his fellow youth pastors around the country often complain of being treated like second-class citizens in their churches. The misconception is that they work less and have more free time than anyone else does, because their work is with students — it looks like too much fun to be work! As a result, youth ministers often receive 1) a lower pay scale than the rest of the pastoral staff, and 2) all the busy work no one else wants to do. This is crazy! Instead of thinking of the youth workers as lowly servants, we should all be looking for ways to reward them for their work and to make sure they know they are an important part of our churches. The only exception is, if you hired a lazy spud! If so, you're stuck. Make him do the busywork until he quits. Good riddance!

Why would anyone think that youth pastors have more free time than the rest of us? The vast majority of the youth pastors I have known have been hard-working servants. Because of the demands of working with young people, they actually have little extra time for menial tasks (though they always seem to make time if asked). Youth pastors keep the latest hours, get up before anyone else, volunteer more of their time, and invest more of themselves into the lives of others. Of course, it makes sense to me that youth pastors would be the hardest working, because they are in the business of raising young men and women to become the next generation of church members and leaders, and that is one of the most difficult tasks I can think of.

This being the case, I think we should compensate youth pastors the same way we do the other top people on our staffs. At New Life, all of us on the pastoral staff are on the same pay scale. The youth pastor, worship pastor, and senior pastor all start at the same rate, and we receive the same percentage raises.

In our weekly staff meetings, I always try to make a point of tuning in to how John is responding to the conversation. If he is being quiet and I can tell something is on his mind, I'll ask, "Okay, John, what are you thinking?" Nine times out of ten, John has something valuable on his mind, and we all benefit from what he has to say. But regardless of what he is thinking, my encouraging him to join the conversation reminds him that his opinion is valuable to me. He knows I never hold him in low regard. In fact, he knows I think of him as being one of the most valuable people in our church.

the importance of friendship

If you want your youth pastor to be innovative and effective, you've got to be his friend. You can't control him, intentionally hurt his feelings, or make him feel unwanted. Never micro-manage, and always make sure he knows he is a vital part of your life. Gayle and I make our pastoral staff part of our family, and for that reason, we often have members of our team over for Christmas and New Year's, have gone on vacations with them, and have spent long weekends together.

A senior pastor I was talking to recently told me that his youth pastor had completely destroyed his church. When I asked how, the senior pastor explained that the youth pastor had sexually molested a child in the community and the aftermath had left the church in shambles. I sympathized with the senior pastor, but then I asked him if he had known his youth pastor was struggling with sexual temptation in this area. Surprised, the senior pastor replied that he had no idea.

In my opinion, this church was destroyed because of the senior pastor's lack of knowledge. We pastors need to take the initiative to befriend one another to avoid situations like this. Everyone is tempted at some time in their lives, and the Bible provides ways for us to successfully deal with temptation so it never has to destroy ministry in the community.

This is one of the reasons why I don't want any secrets among my staff. I make a point to always look into my youth pastors eyes, not as his superior, but as his friend. If I detect any shame, depression, or anxiety, I'll take him to lunch or somewhere we can talk privately. Once alone, I'll ask him what is wrong. Sometimes he'll say, "Ted, this is a personal issue. I don't want to talk about it." Then I'll say, "Okay, what kind of personal issue?"

The point is, I don't talk to my youth pastor like he is one of my employees, or like he is the person responsible for making sure families stay in the church. He is my friend, my co-worker, and my partner in ministry and in life. I am concerned for the things that concern him and I truly want to see God's best for him every day.

eight ways to befriend your youth pastor and ensure a strong youth program

1. Love them. Be concerned for their good.

2. Go on a missions trip or to a ministry conference together. This provides a wonderful opportunity for the two of you to grow together through common experiences and learning new ideas together. This also gives you opportunities to read your Bibles and pray together, which will strengthen your spiritual bond.

3. Have some fun together.

4. Protect them. Make sure they take adequate time off and have their needed family time. Defend them from unreasonable demands or judgments coming from people in the congregation, and do things to insure that they know they are valuable to you.

5. Keep them on your same pay scale and look for unique ways to bless them.

6. Maintain an "air of affirmation" by publicly reminding the church what a great job the youth department is doing.

7. Take the time to know your youth pastor's strengths and weaknesses. Capitalize on their strengths and work with the weaknesses.

8. Give your youth pastor plenty of OPPORTUNITY to grow, to fail, and to dream. When they fail, coach a little bit. When they succeed, acknowledge and encourage their success.

Certainly, these eight ideas will help in developing a strong youth program in your church. However, good youth ministry requires a lot more than just incentive and friendship. It also requires good people. They have to know you, your calling, and your vision, and have the personal character necessary to mold their own lives into a team.

Although I don't specifically look for unusual academic training, three out of the four guys currently serving in our youth ministry have professional degrees outside of their areas of service. John Bolin graduated as a marketing major and worked for several years in secular business. Brad Parsley, our associate youth pastor, has a degree in music and directed a nationally known music group before being scooped up by New Life Church. In addition to leading one of the largest Junior High ministries in the Rocky Mountain region, he is now using his degree in music to train a youth choir of more than one hundred young people. Christopher Beard, our Internship Director, has his undergraduate degree in business and a graduate degree in Christian counseling with an emphasis in child psychology. Where most young men with his education are working in treatment facilities, he is taking the brightest and best high school graduates from around the country and training them to be mentally alert, physically strong, socially magnetic, and spiritually alive. In addition to practical life skills and professionalism, all of our youth pastors are continually educating themselves to become experts in adolescent development, the Word, and the power of God.

Where do we find good young people? Three places to look are: 1) in your own churches, 2) through Christian colleges and universities, and 3) through Christian organizations on or near secular university campuses. If we are in need of someone for our team and can't find them within our church, then either I or someone from my staff will schedule a time of ministry in or near college campuses. While there, our primary purpose isn't for the ministry opportunity itself, but rather to meet humble, godly young men and women who love God, love people, and are willing to minister through local church ministry. I never announce that I'm looking for staff members, but instead, make myself as available as possible to meet Christian students, and trust that one of them will stand out to me. Some always do. There are always great young men and women looking for opportunities to minister in a healthy environment.

The years of allowing a love-starved, twenty-something, overweight, undereducated, volunteer to coordinate our ministry to young people is long past. We have transitioned into a time when we need to attract and keep the sharpest and best young men and women in our community to minister to our young people. When we do that, we attract strong families, we can model godly living to those in need, and our churches will grow, because of the strength of our ministries to the young people of our communities. Our young people deserve it.

chapter four

Many of us hear the statistics — the divorces, the broken homes, the unwanted pregnancies, guns and drugs in schools — but we don't really understand the personal side which we're about to see in this chapter. This is the heartbeat of young America — the plight of today's teens. You get a chance to peer into their world, and in addition, you can see how parents and leaders can reach in and make a real difference.

We're not talking about a bunch of young people with weird hair, weird clothes, and weird attitudes we can never relate to. They are human beings going through many phases that are normal, just like you and I went through, but with different expressions. This generation is special. God has a divine plan for each young person alive. Let God begin to melt your heart with compassion as you read this chapter.

ron

a tribe apart
by jay strack

The twists and turns of a generation are not a bad thing, but merely a fact of life. Yet there is something deeply disturbing about the spiritual dryness and barrenness of our most cherished possessions — our children. Unfortunately, we have no one to blame but ourselves. As I've gazed into the faces of literally millions of teenagers, it reminds me of watching the ocean and sensing that there is something lurking just underneath the surface. Suddenly, without warning, a fin appears. Does it appear merely for a second or two and then reappear fifty yards away? Will it turn out to be a playful, harmless dolphin, or is it the steady, constant fin of a dangerous shark?

I want to be very practical on how the Church can reach and keep what has been called the Millennial Generation. I prefer to refer to them as the Digital Generation, or the N-GEN.

Reaching them is not an option. It is later than we think. The time has long passed for debating and dialogues. It is time for reveille — a call to arms. Before the Church can put on the outer armor, we must settle some issues in our hearts. We must determine, as pastors and parents, policemen and principals, what are primary issues and what are secondary issues. The consequences are too great and the needs of this generation are too urgent to play games. We can no longer give the appearance that we have written off this generation, but by our attitude, as well as our actions, we have given that very appearance.

The youth of our day have the perception that those of us in leadership positions, whether on a national level or in the local church or school, don't like the way they look or the way they dress; we don't like their tattoos or their body piercing; we don't like the color of their hair, their music, or anything about them. And guess what? It shows! I'm more than convinced that our displeasure is beyond perception — it is a reality.

Eighty-eight percent of this generation, twenty-nine and under, do not go to a church, a synagogue, a parish, or an assembly hall for any type of spiritual exposure. Nothing, nada, zip — 88 percent! Sadly, not many are troubled by that fact.

jay strack

The youth of our day have the perception that those of us in leadership positions, whether on a national level or in the local church or school, don't like the way they look or the way they dress; we don't like their tattoos or their body piercing; we don't like the color of their hair, their music, or anything about them. And guess what? It shows! I'm more than convinced that our displeasure is beyond perception — it is a reality.

But there is another statistic that should break our heart and bring every one of us to our knees in prayer. Between 85 and 88 percent of all those who have been raised in our churches are not coming back to church when they graduate from high school. Obviously, this survey and the statistical evidence has not mapped out these young people throughout all their lives. We don't know what happens when they turn forty and are faced with the realities of life. They may very well find themselves back in church. While it has proven true in previous times, there's always evidence that those, once they have several children and have experienced the heaviness of life, will begin to try to find their way back to church. But I'm talking about once young people are on their own, 88 percent of those raised in our churches are not coming back to church. In essence, we are reaching 12 percent of the 12 percent.

Don't ever forget this phrase, "If we keep doing what we're doing, we're going to keep having what we're having."

I believe this generation has become a tribe apart. I believe that if we would have shown the same concern for this generation as we would any other unreached people, group, or tribe, we might not have alienated as many of them.

But when he saw the multitudes, he was moved with compassion on them, because they fainted, and were scattered abroad, as sheep having no shepherd.
Then saith he unto his disciples, The harvest truly is plenteous, but the labourers are few;
Pray ye therefore the Lord of the harvest, that he will send forth labourers into his harvest.

Matthew 9:36-38

This shows the heart of Jesus as He saw the people — sheep without a shepherd. He paints a picture of the sheep being chased by a pack of wolves — bleating, wandering, lost, and totally exhausted. This is a precise picture of today's generation. If we saw them this way, it would break our hearts. Our young people are as sheep without a shepherd.

I'm afraid we have yet to view this generation in the same way they see themselves. As we used to say when I spent years on the street, we need to "size up" this generation. We need to listen to them. We need to find out where they are coming from. We must take time to get involved with them and learn all about them. I believe as much as anything that when we care enough to have a relationship with a young man or young woman, it is going to be a royal pain! But we can't write them off. We must not dismiss them or blow them off. We must care about them and treat them like they're someone special, because they are. I have found that we must love them as a child, but treat them with the respect we would give an adult.

I was really discouraged when I read several of the latest definitive books on this generation, two in particular *(A Tribe Apart* by Patricia Hersch and *Growing Up Digital* by Don Tapscott), that there is not a single solitary reference to the Church or even a reference to Jesus Christ. Another reason why we cannot afford to write them off is that there are more young people alive, eighteen and under, than any other age group, including the baby boomers. And there are more young people alive on this earth today than in any other period — outnumbering even the baby boomers. So I say to you, we can't write off this generation.

Understand that America is not mentioned in biblical prophecy. One of the reasons I believe America is not mentioned is because we may not play a great prominent role at the time of the end. Russia, China, Germany, Asia, Israel, and Iraq are all mentioned. Where's America?

I believe one reason may be because of all the babies who have been aborted in that age group. How many men and women who would have served in our armed forces have we thrown away as a result of selfish interests? Will we have the armies necessary to sufficiently defend our interests at the time of the end? But secondly, I believe there's going to be a generation that perhaps we failed to reach with the Gospel message. Consequently, they don't care about our spiritual heritage or share our spiritual values.

When I am speaking in a stadium, coliseum, or church, I attempt to look deep into the young faces in attendance. Some years ago, while speaking in India, my eyes fell on one particular young girl. Although the left side of her face displayed a pure beauty, the right side was hideously scarred. I knew instantly what had happened. Just a few days earlier, in another village, my heart had lurched with horror over the remains of a young boy who had been ripped apart by an animal of the jungle. At that moment, as if in response to my thoughts, the darkness was split by a terrifying snarl from the surrounding jungle. Dread and fear spread over the faces around me as the roar of the great jungle beast shattered the wind and shook the thatched arbor.

I hear a similar roar today as I examine the clear danger faced by our children as they attempt to walk the treacherous road that leads to adulthood. I am reminded of the "lion" of which the apostle Peter warned so long ago.

> **Be sober, be vigilant; because your adversary the devil, as a roaring lion, walketh about, seeking whom he may devour.**
>
> **1 Peter 5:8**

Since that day in the jungle many years ago, I have spoken to scores of teenagers whose lives have been ripped apart or scarred by their adversary, the devil. Those memories are vividly imprinted in my mind, and I constantly feel the need to warn parents and children that Satan stalks his prey, watching and waiting for the opportunity to pounce.

The word Peter uses for *adversary* is a word for an opponent in a lawsuit. (See James Strong's, *The Exhaustive Concordance of the Bible* (Nashville: Abingdon, 1890), "Greek Dictionary of the New Testament," #476.) Parents must never forget that this enemy will slander and accuse them in the eyes of their own children in an attempt to coerce teens to run ahead or fall behind the protection and care of their families. Satan attacks on all sides, threatening body, soul, mind, and spirit. His attacks have perhaps never been fiercer than in our present age.

In a real sense, today's parents are fighting a fierce battle for their children. As I see it, the battle is raging in four arenas. First is the battle for the mind, which involves the constant assault of anti-Christian values. Second is the battle for the body, which primarily involves sexual sin. Third is the battle for the family, which involves the breakup of homes. Finally, there is the battle for the soul. Never forget that the adversary we face plays for keeps. The ultimate price is for all eternity.

Peter alerts us to the battle for the mind with these urgent words: "Be sober." The word "sober" literally means to have a sound and healthy mind, to guard and protect our thoughts. Picture building a defensive wall around your mind like the massive walls that used to protect cities from invaders. Peter also uses the words, "be vigilant," which means to be morally alert, especially guarding against sexual promiscuity.

The Scripture makes it clear that our thoughts determine the direction of our lives. **As he thinks in his heart, so is he** (Proverbs 23:7 AMP). Since Satan knows this, he daily assaults the hearts and minds of our children with the battering rams of anti-Christian values. Some of these values are even advocated in the schools. The media bombards children with images designed to seduce them away from the teachings of Scripture and common decency. The fruit basket of values offered to children by schools, the media, and home is then mixed together and offered again by their peers. Unfortunately, the values of their peers, who serve as a kind of surrogate parent in the lives of many young people today, often win out over those of their parents and their church.

What messages are our children getting? A thorough examination of the value choices confronting our homes reveals a conflict of visions. The world offers visions of limited importance and a limited future, which, I believe, produce a vision of a limited life.

When we speak of this generation or of kids at risk, perhaps we should put a face on it. We are not speaking arbitrarily about just any young person. We could be speaking about your own children, grandchildren, nieces, or nephews. It could be the young people in your youth group or perhaps your neighbor's children. These young people have a personal adversary who never rests.

This very thought is what led me to start Student Leadership University (SLU) in my hometown of Orlando, Florida, several years ago. After spending twenty years on the road, primarily conducting evangelistic crusades across the country and around the world, I determined to fulfill a God-given vision of implementing leadership skills in the selected "cream of the crop" youth from evangelical churches throughout America. During the summer of 1998, over 1,100 students participated in not only SLU 101 (Orlando), but also in SLU 201 (Washington, D. C.), and SLU 301 (Israel).

During SLU 101, the students are led down three different tracks for five days while visiting Orlando, Florida, one of the tourism capitals of the world. Track One is "Behind the Scenes of Technology," where students experience Sea World's mission to provide world class entertainment while expanding global leadership in environmental education, conservation, and research. Students are also taken behind the scenes at the country's largest working motion picture production facility outside of Hollywood — Universal Studios Florida.

Track Two is the "Leadership Skills" track where I lead the students through the "Capture the Future" seminar, and they also participate in the leading time-management course. This track helps students learn visionary goal-setting, how to get along with difficult people, how to develop the leader within, and the importance of people skills.

Track Three is the "Defending the Faith" track where the SLU faculty, including several Ph.D.'s, conduct seminars on such topics as: "Creation vs. Evolution," "New Age Nonsense," "Moral Issues of the Day — Homosexuality, Abortion, and Moral Purity," and "Beyond the Glitter of Movies, Media, and Music." There is no appropriate way for me to explain how tremendously rewarding it has been to see the transformation that takes place in the lives of the SLU graduates.

Just as we have spared no expense in the number one priority of my ministry, the globally televised project called *The Millennium Chorus* that will usher in the new millennium from an evangelical Christian perspective, we have also committed vast financial resources toward making SLU the finest student leadership experience possible. Both areas have their own website, and I encourage you to investigate both via the Internet. Millennium Chorus' website is www.millenniumchorus.com. Student Leadership University's address is www.studentz.com\slu. The point I want to make is that we should treat the students with the same respect as we would any adult. I have found that they respond in a very positive way.

The whole aim of SLU is to give students the tools to combat their dreaded adversary. He walks to and fro, and he will either scar them for life, or he will tear them to shreds, limb from limb. I believe the purpose of this book is that by the Spirit of Almighty God we would be so altered and so different that we would say, "Over my dead body will the evil one, the malignant one, destroy one of my children, or one of my young people whom God has called me to shepherd!"

I believe that we do not see this generation the way Jesus sees them, and I know we don't see them the way they see themselves. There are several factors why I believe young people truly are a tribe apart.

The Crumbling of the Home

The latest statistics are alarming. Two out of every five white kids, and three out of every five black or Hispanic kids do not even have a man in their house tonight. You may wonder why I break it down in ethnic terms, but it's because I want you to see we're all in this together. When we hear these type of statistics, we always think it's "that other group." I like what my friend, Tony Evans, once said, "We might have all come to this country in different ships, but we're in the same boat today."

We must learn that if there is a problem in the inner city or in one of the impoverished areas with black young people, Hispanic young people, or white young people, it is all our problem. Apparently, many didn't care about the drug epidemic when it affected "those folks"; many shrugged their shoulders at the problem of teenage pregnancy in the inner city; many responded with apathy when there were deaths due to crack cocaine and heroin use in another town; we were not moved to action when hearing about kids growing up without fathers, and many of us really didn't care about the gang problem — until it moved into our neighborhoods.

I'm tired of trying to explain why the Church didn't do this and why we didn't do that. I can't answer why the Church or why society failed to reach out and make a difference in the past, but I must answer for what we do or fail to do today. My prayer is that a light will come on in our heads, and the love of God will be shed abroad in our hearts.

I believe the purpose of this book is that by the Spirit of Almighty God we would be so altered and so different that we would say, "Over my dead body will the evil one, the malignant one, destroy one of my children, or one of my young people whom God has called me to shepherd!"

Only then are we going to say that if something's going on in that home, it's my problem. We are in this together. We must be our brother's keeper.

The first reason for the crumbling of the home is because of the fading of the fathers. I went through six broken homes as a young boy growing up in Florida. Needless to say, I was as confused as a termite in a yo-yo. When I heard the words as a young, teenage junky and a senior in high school, "Jay, God wants to be your heavenly Father," my exact words were (I remember as though it was yesterday), "I think I'll 'el paso' on the father thing." I had already had six. I didn't need another one. Of course, that might explain why I was addicted to speed for four years.

In my opinion, the two most effective campus ministries on the planet are Campus Crusade on the college campuses and First Priority in the high schools and middle schools. The reason they do not go on campus and begin talking a great deal with students about the fatherhood of God is that so many in this generation have had such a negative experience with a father figure in the home that it does more harm than good to mention it. You have to talk about how He's the Creator. You have to talk about how He is the Holy God, He is the Lawgiver, He is the Just One, He is the Righteous One, and He is the Loving One, and then you talk to them about "He is a Father."

I believe Satan has aimed all of his cannons at the home and at the family, because one of the great distinctions of the Christian faith is when Jesus said we could call this all-powerful Creator a loving, intimate *Abba Father.* It rocked the world! **Our Father who art in heaven** (Matthew 6:9 NASB), is such an intimate term. Why would we have a David Koresh? Why would we have a Charles Manson in the sixties? Why would we have a Sun Jung Moon? Why would we have a Jim Jones in the jungles of Guyana? Why do we have all that? The cults are booming, because everyone desires a father and everyone desires a family. They all refer to themselves as *family,* and all of those cults I mentioned call their leader Father or Dad.

Another reason young people are drawn to the cults is because they not only want a father and a family, but they want a future. All of the cults promise their followers a future. You will never understand this generation until you come to the simple conclusion — they are a tribe apart! We may not understand their culture or know

I believe Satan has aimed all of his cannons at the home and at the family, because one of the great distinctions of the Christian faith is when Jesus said we could call this all-powerful Creator a loving, intimate *Abba Father.* It rocked the world! **Our Father who art in heaven** (Matthew 6:9 NASB), is such an intimate term.

why they think the way they think. We have a real problem with almost everything they do and almost everything they stand for, but you need to understand that this is a lonely generation, and they are as confused as a lost lamb when it comes to love, life, and relationships.

When I started at nineteen, I never dreamed that at the age of forty-two I would still preach to high school students, much less still relate to them. I started out as one of them, kind of like a big brother and a friend, and now, I could be their father! I have spoken in over 9,000 public schools, and I tell students this: Don't ever skip church. Don't ever skip school. If you do, God will get you. I'm in church every night of my life, and I'm in school all day, every day. God will get you!

Why is it Josh McDowell, with all his gray hair, can still hold teenagers captive when he speaks? It is because Josh loves them and relates to them as a father figure. Kids are hungry for a father. You'll never understand this generation's rebellion, resentment, restlessness, anger, aloofness, and distance until you understand this fact.

You look at them and they've got doll eyes. They're having to teach children at the age of three and four to cry, because all their lives as babies they cried and never got a response. We have a generation that doesn't even know how to cry out to their father and, in turn, get a loving response. This is the generation of the absentee fathers.

Secondly, there is the melting of the mothers. Almost every magazine aimed at women stresses how to be sexy, how to climb the corporate ladder, and how to be fulfilled physically, emotionally, financially. This appears to be the emphasis of today, but there's hardly any emphasis on how to be a godly mom, how to love those babies, and how to take care of their children and live for them.

When you have the fading of the fathers and the melting of the mothers, you have the crying of the children. This generation cries themselves to sleep every night. I ask you, pastors, youth ministers, missionaries, professors, and evangelists: How many more nights are we going to go to bed dry-eyed when everyone around us seems to be crying themselves to sleep?

When I speak in high schools, many times I go from one school to another without actually getting to speak to the students on a one-on-one basis. How do you walk away from fifteen, twenty, or thirty girls or guys weeping and sobbing? It is almost unbearable.

Without question, there is the crumbling of the home. At the end of each school day, hundreds of kids in your community, whom your church should be reaching, go home with a key in their hand, they open the door, they shut that door, and no one else is there. It's their world alone!

In a recent study sponsored by the Carnegie Counsel called "Turning Points," an incredible statement was given. It said, "Half of all American youth are at risk for serious problems — substance abuse, early unprotected sex, dangerous activities, dropouts, and delinquent behavior." Fifty percent of America's youth are at risk of never even reaching the age of twenty-one. Another study, "The Troubled Journey," makes this startling revelation when it says, "America has forgotten how to raise healthy children." This is the crumbling of the home.

A Crisis in the Classroom

I have been speaking in schools for twenty-four years, and never thought I would have to walk through metal detectors or have policemen escort me into the school buildings. It's not unusual to be handed a handful of pills or handful of joints while on a school campus. I am privileged to have a young man named Charles Billingsly sing in all our crusades, but before Charles joined us, I had a gentleman on my team named Jack Price. Jack Price is in his fifties, and a tremendously gifted choral director and soloist. He's as conservative as you get, and after one crusade in Atlanta, a young man walked up to him and said, "Would you give this to Jay Strack?" Jack Price took what the guy handed him and carried it with him as he left for his home in Texas. He put it on the conveyor belt that went through the Atlanta airport and, with no one stopping him, carried it all the way through. He gave me what the young man had given him a few days later in my Dallas office — a crack pipe with about $100 worth of crack in it. Here is Jack Price walking through the airports with enough illegal drugs to have had him put behind bars for years. I was extremely grateful (and so was Jack) for God's protection!

However, who protects this generation from the crisis in the classroom? Who is there to guard them against the drugs and violence they face every day of their lives? Where is the Church?

• The Corruption of the Culture

Many kids today are being raised by adults who are still trying to find themselves. I was privileged to serve on three presidential drug task forces. While serving on one several years ago, I attended a big meeting held at the Indian Treaty Room at the White House. All the muckety-mucks were there from CNN and the other media sources. It was exciting to be at the all-day meeting with a reception to be held that night.

I was shocked when I walked into the reception hall later that evening and saw all the ladies in low-cut gowns, and most of the men who had been involved in the earlier meetings on our nation's drug problem with a cigarette in one hand and a drink in the other. In addition, many of the guys were jockeying for position to get a good angle of the ladies in the low-cut gowns.

Later, they had the audacity to address once again the drug problem in America and were asking what needed to be done. I thought they actually wanted an answer. Oh boy, was I ever wrong! I spoke up and said, "Well, I've got an answer," and they all looked at me. I went on, "I'll tell you what we need to do. First of all, you ladies need to go put a sweater on, and you guys need to quit standing on your tongue, put the cigarette out, and pour the cocktail out. You do that, and we can reach this generation of young people. But you can't play games!"

Alcohol is in 70 percent of the homes in America. Our churches are full of "sipping saints." I have a hat in my study that was given to me at the R. J. Reynolds High School that was built by R. J. Reynolds, the tobacco mogul. During the assembly program there, I spoke for thirty minutes about the hazards and pitfalls of smoking. I just can't help it when there is so much corruption and hypocrisy in our American culture.

We have a generation of adults trying to squeeze their children into their busy schedules. I don't believe there has ever been a generation that's gone through so much social change. I was the contributing editor for the "True Love Waits" Youth Bible, but many of the N-GEN youth culture have a new definition for sex. There is a game played by young people that involves not only intercourse, but something called outercourse. That's a far cry from virtue. What has happened to this culture? The decay must truly nauseate our Holy God.

Coldness in the Church

Think with me for a moment about duct tape. A recent study conducted by scientists at Lawrence Berkeley National Laboratory in San Jose, California, reports that duct tape has thousands of uses. There's just one problem — it doesn't work on air conditioning or heating ducts! This silvery substance does everything but what it was invented to do.

The analogy is self-apparent among many of today's ministers. It seems we do everything. Most of us don't get enough sleep, but when we go to bed, there are people still upset that we haven't done enough! Ministers can't be any busier or work any harder, but we better start working smarter. We're doing everything except the very thing we are called to do — reach this generation for Jesus. I don't care how you do it, just do it!

There is a large, prominent church in Florida that believes any song written after 1950 cannot be sung in their church. They have no contemporary music at all, but they reach hundreds of teenagers. Then you go to another church, and it's "pump up the volume and rip off the knob." They also reach hundreds of teenagers. Do you know what they both have in common? *They love teenagers.* Now, we have to make certain we are honoring God's calling and will for our life and ministry when we conduct the work of the Church, but let's do *something!* Let's not be like the duct tape, never doing what we were designed to do. Let's not be the coldness in the Church.

In Tampa, Florida, there's a tragic story of three teenagers who got bored and decided to collect signs for the trailer they were living in. One person thought an alligator crossing sign was cool, so they cut it down. Another teenager cut down a school zone sign to put where they all did their homework. Another one, who was mad at one of the guys she was living with, wanted to put "stop" on her door, so they took a stop sign.

About an hour later, four other teenagers, good kids, coming home from a school function, minding their own business, sober, straight, and everything you would want your young person to be, ran through the intersection where normally there was a stop sign and were killed in a car wreck. Four teenagers lost their lives because someone took down the stop sign! This is what's wrong with this generation. Whether it be the school, the home, and sometimes the local church, it seems as though we have taken down all the signs. Our kids have no signs left to warn them and protect them against the dangers that lie in their paths.

One of the most moving stories I've read in some time is of a young lady who was deaf. She petitioned the court to remove her from her father's care so she could be placed in the care of the lady who interpreted for her at school. Her mother had left years earlier with another man, because the deaf girl was too much trouble. The husband stayed to raise the daughter, but now she was sixteen years old, and in all those years, the father had never learned one word of sign language. The young girl wept and said, "I want to be with someone who wants to talk to me."

The judge brought the father up on stage and irately asked him, "Why have you never bothered?"

The father replied, "I don't know what the big deal is. If I want her attention, all I have to do is pound on something, scream at the top of my lungs, or throw something." I'm afraid some of us think the only way to reach this generation is to pound the pulpit a little harder and raise our voice a little louder, but I'm convinced that's not what it's going to take to reach this generation. We can't afford to have a coldness in our churches any longer.

I believe there are three things you have to be to reach this generation. First, you've got to be *real*. Recently, I returned a call made to me by a young evangelist. The answering service referred to this young man's office as an "international ministry." I knew he had been to only one country outside of the United States. That's the kind of nonsense that causes young people to write us off. Young people have 20/20 vision when it comes to spotting a phony, but they're blind as a bat when it comes to detecting their own phoniness. Sounds a whole lot like many adults. If you want to reach this generation, you and I have got to be real. Is there anything more tragic than some middle-aged man trying to dress and act young, or for that matter a middle-aged woman trying to dress and act like someone half her age? Young people want you to be who you are and not something or someone else. If you want to reach this generation, be real.

It is important for you to realize that this generation isn't demanding that you be just like them. You don't have to look like them, you don't have to dress like them, you don't have to talk like them, and you don't have to like their music. They'll accept you just like you are if you act just like you are. But they know you won't accept them like they are if you're trying to be something you're not. You've got to be real.

Not too long ago, I was in one of the largest churches of my own denomination. There were over 3,000 young people present for a big youth night. We had been in all the schools, God had blessed, and the turnout was absolutely tremendous. One of the deacons came running into the pastor's study and proclaimed to the pastor, "There's over 3,000 kids out there!"

The pastor said, "Isn't that great? That's what we've been asking God for."

The deacon replied, "Well, preacher, you don't understand. They're wearing hats!"

They're wearing hats! Suddenly, I was deeply troubled. I jumped up and I said, "They're wearing hats?!"

The deacon sensed I was being a little facetious and said, "This is serious, preacher! They've got their hats on backwards!"

Oh, well, now that was different! That's where we've got to draw the line, baby!

Don't young people need to be taught that when they come into the house of God they shouldn't wear a hat? Of course, they do. Do they need to be taught that God's house is holy and sacred? Of course, they do. But there's something wrong when we can't rejoice that there are hundreds or even thousands of kids in attendance, and all we think about is that they have a hat on. Let's concentrate on getting Jesus into their heart and counseling with them first. We'll worry about their hats later.

I'm afraid we have "Sergeant Slaughter," and others like him, placed in key positions in our churches. Why don't we have the courage to remove them? Wake up, people! Most of our parking lot attendants are like the Gadarene demoniac. They are never in Sunday school. They just roam around, and if you don't go where they are waving, they'll pound on your hood with that flashlight and demand you go the way they want.

Let me give you another example. Who do we have counseling in our churches? Once, at one of our crusades, a man said to a young boy weeping at the altar, "You get rid of that junk in your ears and look like a man, then I'll talk to you." Now there are body parts of that man that still have not been found. Read this carefully. It doesn't matter if Sergeant Slaughter likes the earring in the kid's ear. It doesn't matter at that moment what he likes or dislikes. What matters is that we give these young people the only hope they will ever have. Our biggest problems are the kids who have been raised in our churches and want to look like all those other kids. This isn't a game. It's time to remove the coldness.

> **But when he saw the multitudes, he was moved with compassion on them, because they fainted, and were scattered abroad, as sheep having no shepherd.**
> **Then saith he unto his disciples, The harvest truly is plenteous, but the labourers are few;**
> **Pray ye therefore the Lord of the harvest, that he will send forth labourers into his harvest.**
> **Matthew 9:36-38**

Why do we continue to do what we do? Primarily, we don't look at young people the way Jesus does. If you picture the verse saying, "They are like sheep without a shepherd. They are faint and can't take another step. They can't go on. They're about to pass out with exhaustion," it would be a picture of little baby lambs wandering all alone. If I could paint what that verse says on a huge piece of canvas, there would be little lambs all by themselves, because dad is gone and mom is gone — they're all alone.

One of the latest studies reveals that many young people today spend 50 percent of their time on their own with no adult supervision. No wonder they look, act, and live the way they do. Do you want to see these kids the way Jesus sees them? Picture the little lambs all by themselves. There would be one bleeding, because it crawled through the cactus or through the thistles to get away from the claws or the jaws of a predator. After all, there is no shepherd to protect it. There would be another lamb dragging its leg, because it was fleeing for its life, got too far out on the cliff, and rolled all the way down to the bottom, breaking its leg in the fall. You see, when Jesus painted that picture of the multitude, it was a picture of those who could not go on. I promise you that if we could ever see teenagers the way Jesus sees teenagers, they would look at us and say, "There's a lady who's real. There is a man who's real." You've got to be real.

Secondly, you've got to be *relevant* to the youth of today. Don't preach a sermon or a Bible study message or deliver a youth challenge unless you can answer the question, "So what?" Your message has to be relevant in the minds of young people. You've got to be real. You've got to be relevant.

Thirdly, you've got to be *relational*. My whole ministry is centered around the big event. People bring me in and we do the big events. It is becoming increasingly harder and harder to do, because young people are relational. They crave relationships. Just remember one word: *process*. It is a process to reach these kids today. There are times we'll see a supernatural transformation take place in a young person's life, but for the most part, that transformation involves a steady process.

Why do I believe in the supernatural power of God? During my senior year in high school, I went into a Bible study as a junky. I had no shirt on, wore cut-off Levi jeans, sandals, and no socks. I was using ninety dollars worth of methamphetornine crystal a day. I had been written off by everyone in my school, my home, and my community.

But I walked out of that Bible study different — changed in a moment, because of the supernatural power of God.

However, there is a process we must not forsake. We must be relational. It may take you five or six attempts at having a relationship with a young person to even get them into the Bible study or to get them to come to your church, but it's worth it — they're worth it. Through your relationships with young people, they will see you are real, they will see you care about them, they will begin to trust you, and they will eventually want what you have — Jesus.

I believe there are eight great issues facing today's generation. I want to discuss a few of them.

Peer Pressure
Relationships
Overall Attitude
Boredom
Learning Disabilities
Esteem
Mind and Mood Altering Drugs
Sex

Don't put down these young people for caving in to peer pressure when they are the most alone, unattached, unsupervised generation that has ever existed. No wonder they crave the gang. No wonder they crave their peers. No wonder they're so hungry to be with the herd or the pack.

I can honestly admit that I hated alcohol as a kid growing up. It had cost me my mom and my dad. My mom even gave away my older brother as a result of alcohol. It made our life a living hell, and I swore I would never drink. But that Friday night, when a guy walked up to me when I was in the seventh grade with the football team and said, "Jay, if you don't want to be with us, go home to your mama." I didn't want to go home, because there was never anyone there. I wanted to be with them, and to be with them I had to drink. To stay with them I had to drink the drink, smoke the joint, and pop the pill. How dare we blast these kids for giving in to peer pressure when our youth groups are so cliquish, so cold, and so standoffish. The most staggering, stunning challenge these kids face that no other generation has faced is *aloneness,* and that is why they will be called the digital generation. They may feel all alone in their school, their home, and their neighborhood, but they can get on the Internet and everyone takes them seriously.

My oldest daughter, Melissa, who is hearing impaired, has such a great attitude. Many times, her peers will say something she can't quite understand, and her response will cause either laughter or ridicule. Even with a 75 percent hearing ability, she sometimes doesn't quite get the message as it was intended. Young people can be cruel at times, but Melissa can get on the Internet and have conversations with five people at one time. This generation realizes they don't have to be alone anymore, especially with the Internet so accessible. Why are our kids flocking the chat rooms on the Internet when that is what our youth groups and churches are supposed to be providing?

It is very important to teach, by example, proper relationships. If you're going to reach this generation, you have to help them not only learn how to have relationships, you've got to establish relationships with them.

I was labeled as having Attention Deficit Disorder Deliberately (ADDD) while in elementary school. ADDD is what best described me. I never bothered anyone — I just sat there.

Some preachers have a hard time with the esteem issue. But as a young person, when you've been alone 50 percent of the time and you're told you're stupid, you're a loser, you're not very bright, and you'll never amount to anything, it has a profound impact on you. I have a man on my staff, Mike Ruth, who is a seminary graduate. I have known him for over twenty years, and we have worked together as partners for eleven of those twenty years. He is one of the finest men on the planet. Recently, we were having lunch and I noticed that he moved all his beans to one side. I said, "Man, don't you like beans?" He said, "Yes, I like beans, but I don't want to talk about it." Since I don't let anyone off the hook, I said, "You're not getting away with that. Why aren't you eating your beans?" He answered, "All of my life my dad told me I would never amount to a hill of beans." Now here's a man who has successfully raised his children and is a wonderful, incredible man of God and a seminary-trained minister, and this is what's still on his mind, "All of my life my old man said I would never amount to a hill of beans." How sad, but true, that harsh, cruel words spoken over children and young people will usually stay with them for the rest of their lives.

Years ago, I was at the Crippled Children's Hospital in Dallas. My daughter, Melissa, received several surgeries there, and I never will forget the time one of the nurses came by and asked, "Dr. Strack, would you walk around and let some of the other kids meet you?" I was being humble and honest when I said, "Well, these kids won't know who I am." She said, "Oh no, I know you will be a stranger," but she said, "I just want them to see a father here." I asked, "What are you talking about?" There are many Crippled Children's Hospitals around the nation, and the head nurse told me that over 85 percent of all the children in the Crippled Children's Hospitals have had their dads bail out on them when they found out their kids would not be the football star, the beauty queen, or the cheerleader. I don't think I've ever been as ashamed of being a man in all my life as I was at that point.

What message are we giving our children? If we don't see them as being important, how do we expect them to see themselves as important? How do we expect them to grow up to be mighty men and women of God, if we don't see them that way to begin with?

If God be for us, who can be against us?

Romans 8:31

This scripture is so powerful. God wants to be our father — a father who will never leave us or forsake us. (See Deuteronomy 31:6.)

There was an emperor by the name of Shah Jahan. He fell deeply in love with a beautiful young princess and married her. He described himself as the happiest man ever to live. And then she died suddenly. He was so grief stricken that all he thought about was taking his own life. Because he was a ruler, he knew that wouldn't be the right thing to do, so he decided to build a monument of love to his beloved, something the whole world would talk about. He found the choicest parcel of land, put her coffin right in the middle, and said, "I'm going to build one of the greatest monuments of love ever constructed."

He got his finest builder and his finest craftsman to draw up the blueprints. After viewing them, he said, "This is it." The days of construction turned into weeks, the weeks into months, and the months into years. The passion became an obsession as he started building what we call the Taj Mahal.

Months later, obsessed with building this great memory to the love of his life, with drawings in his hand, he ran by a pile of lumber and tools with weeds growing up around it, having no idea what it was. He tripped and fell, cutting a huge gash in his leg. In the anger and the pain of the moment, he looked at the pile that was so inconveniently in his way, and said, "Whatever that is, get it out of here! Remove it!" His loyal followers did whatever he commanded, so they cleared away the entire pile. Sadly, the emperor had no idea that the object of his affection, the very one all of this was supposed to be for, was discarded. You see, one day someone set a tool down on the coffin, just for a moment. A few days later someone threw a piece of scrap wood on top, and over the months of construction, other people added their discards to the growing pile. Soon, time and weeds overtook the emperor's very object of his affection as he busied himself with trying to finish his great monument of love. Sometime during the construction process, the emperor lost the passion for his beloved to only the memory.

The passion of our life when we started training and we started the ministry was Jesus Christ. Remember when we first wept, and said, "Lord, I will do what You want me to do. I'll do it the way You want me to do it. I want to see people the way You see people." But something happens to us along the way and somehow the object of our affection gets so easily discarded.

In times like these, we desperately need Teen Mania-type conferences, of which I have been privileged to be a part of across the country. These conferences are one of the most effective tools I have seen in not only reaching this generation, but helping thousands more "acquire the fire." May we once again reclaim that daily devotion and that first love that challenges us to see others as Jesus sees them. Only then will you and I portray the life and speak the words that will win this generation to Christ. No doubt, with the world at its worst, we who name the matchless name of Jesus must be at our best. We must be His best!

IMPACTING THIS GENERATION

section two

chapter five

Many of our young people today are wandering around all through their teenage years trying to figure out what life's all about, why they were born, and whether they're saved or unsaved. In fact, a recent statistic says that 35 percent of all born-again people are still trying to find the meaning of life. As parents, pastors, youth pastors, leaders, and people who care about young people, it's our responsibility to help them find a purpose. It's our job to help them be in a position where they can hear God's voice and do what they were born to do. It's our mandate to help them discover their fullest potential and live up to it. We are to challenge, encourage, inspire, and lift them to the next highest level.

Whether it's the teenagers in your house who are of your own lineage or the young people in your church, whether it's the young people down the street from you or your children's friends, instead of just leaving them out in the cold and hoping they can figure out their own purpose and "what to do with their life," we need to mentor them, encourage them, and coach them so they're not like the rest of the world. They get the attitude that they're losers and never figure out what to do with their life, and we act like it's not our responsibility. But with our help, they'll discover early in life what they were born to do and get a glimpse of their potential. They will feel us, as their parents and leaders, constantly nudging them out of the nest to soar like an eagle and fulfill their greatest potential.

ron

finding purpose and maximizing potential

by myles munroe

Where there is no vision, the people perish: but he that keepeth the law, happy is he.

Proverbs 29:18

The greatest tragedy in life is not death, but life without a reason. It is dangerous to be alive and not know why you were given life.

From the beginning of man's history as we know it, mankind has been grappling with the age-old questions: Why am I here? What is the reason for my existence? What is the meaning of my life? Is there a reason for the universe, the creation, and man? These questions are universal. They lurk deep within the secret chambers of every human being on earth, regardless of their race, color, ethnic heritage, socio-economic status, or nationality. Philosophers such as Plato, Aristotle, Socrates, and others throughout the ages have attempted to explore these seemingly illusive questions. For the most part, their efforts have ended in more questions than answers.

The deepest craving of the human spirit is to find a sense of significance and relevance. This internal passion is what motivates and drives every human being, either directly or indirectly. It directs his decisions, controls his behavior, and dictates his responses to his environment.

This need for significance is the cause of great tragedies. Many suicides owe their manifestation to this compelling need. Many mass murderers and serial killers confess the relationship of their anti-social behavior to their need to feel important or to experience a sense of self-worth.

This passion for relevance and a sense of significance makes one race or ethnic group elevate itself above another. It also gives birth to prejudice and causes the fabrication of erroneous perceptions that result in grave injustices and the conception of abominable dreams and inhuman behavior.

This desperate desire to feel important and relevant to one's existence also causes the sacrifice of common sense, good judgment, moral standards, and basic human values. Many individuals have sacrificed excellent reputations and years of character building lifestyles for the sake of advancement to a desired position, or a place of recognition and fame in their society or workplace, so they can feel important and worthwhile.

In essence, this deep desire and drive for a sense of importance, significance, and relevance is the cause and the motivator of all human behavior and conflict. This passion for significance knows no boundaries. Rich and poor are victims of its power. King and peasant suffer under its rule. This yearning for relevance and significance is evidence of an internal vacuum in the nature of all mankind, young and old, that needs to be filled. This age-old passion is the pursuit of purpose, a relentless reaching for a reason for the gift of life.

purpose is the key to life

"Let me go. Please let me die," sobbed the frail, old gentleman as the strong, young swimmer struggled against the boisterous waves of the open ocean.

"Just a few more minutes, sir, and I will have you safely to shore," replied the young man, gasping for every breath.

Finally they made it to the beach and both fell, desperately exhausted, onto the sand. "Why did you save me?" cried the angry, seventy-six-year-old man. "Why didn't you let me die? Your good deed is the curse of my existence."

Startled by these words, the young man looked down at the older man who had nearly drowned. As he panted from the heroic effort of rescuing the victim from the violent waves, he shook his head, revealing the shock and the mystification that filled his mind.

Winston had known Mr. Cambridge for twenty years, and had always admired the hard-working businessman for his success. Having worked all his life to achieve the status of being the wealthiest man in the city, Mr. Cambridge owned millions of dollars worth of investments and an enviable mansion on the beach front. He was the father of three well-educated children who all worked in his companies, and the husband of a woman who loved him. Hundreds of friends, relatives, and admirers looked to him for inspiration and guidance. Perplexed by the disparity between his observations of Mr. Cambridge's life and the gentleman's desire to die, Winston asked, "But, sir, why do you want to die?"

As tears flooded his aged eyes, the old man buried his face in his hands and lamented, "What was it all for? Is this all there is? What did I gain? I have everything and yet nothing. Everyone thinks I am a success, but I am a failure. I have given everything and received nothing. I made my parents happy and proud of me, and my wife has everything she could desire. My children want for nothing, and my reputation among my friends, associates, and enemies is impressive. Still, I am empty, depressed, frustrated, and sad. My life has no meaning. Unlike my bank accounts, which are well filled, I am unfulfilled.

"Everyone knows *what* I am, but I still don't know *why* I am. For years, I have been so driven by the expectations of others that I have not discovered my personal reason for being. I do not wish to live with such emptiness. Today, I decided it was better to be dead than to be alive and not know *why.*"

These words pierced the younger man's soul. As he attempted to regain his composure, the old man took his hand, looked into his eyes with a soul-searching gaze, and said, "Son, do not strive to be like me. Find out who you are and be *yourself.*"

As the medics carried the old man away, young Winston stood staring out to sea. The old man's words had stirred him deeply. "Who am I? What does it mean to be myself?" echoed in his brain.

These questions — Who am I? Why am I here? Where did I come from? What was I born to do? Where do I fit? Why am I different? Where am I going? — are haunting our young people. They must realize that purpose is the key to enjoying a meaningful, effective, and fulfilling life. There are millions today just like Mr. Cambridge. They are busy making a living, but they experience very little of life. If your vision for life is measured by status, your upkeep will be your downfall. Vision is buried in purpose. Without knowledge of purpose, life becomes an endless string of activities with little or no significance.

There are young people in every nation who seem to have lost their sense of purpose. They are out of touch with the values, morals, and convictions that build strong families, secure communities, healthy societies, and prosperous nations.

History shows that the value of life decreases and the quality of existence diminishes when a generation loses its sense of destiny and purpose. A quick glance at our current world exposes a sad picture that demands our attention. We are teaching our children to preserve nature, for example, but kill babies. We want smarter students, but are they wiser? In our rushed society, we go faster but get nowhere, and of the time that seems to vanish, little of it is spent on our young people. We instill in them the importance of conquering space, but cannot even conquer our own habits.

King Solomon's words contain principles that every person should heed. Where there is no purpose, there is no self-control, no moral conviction, and no ethical boundaries. (See Proverbs 29:18.) This principle is increasingly evident in both our personal and corporate lives. America spends more money annually on drugs than on oil. The "Land of the Free and the Home of the Brave" has become the world's number one addict.

The famous television producer/writer Norman Lear, when commenting on the disillusionment in America, said, "The societal disease of our time is short-term thinking." In essence, we have lost our long-term vision and our sense of destiny. Where there is no purpose, no internal reason for living, and no significance in life, the demand for discipline, commitment, self-control, and respect for authority will gradually diminish until we, like Mr. Cambridge, will sit among our lifelong accomplishments and cry with regret, "Is this all there is?"

Young people must realize that their fulfillment in life is dependent on them becoming and doing what they were born to be and do. Anything less is not of God.

Therefore I do not run like a man running aimlessly; I do not fight like a man beating the air.

1 Corinthians 9:26 NIV

pushing in the wrong direction

It was the moment for which everyone had been waiting all evening. The thunderous applause of the excited crowd filled the air after the mayor made the announcement, "Ladies and gentlemen, it gives me great pleasure to present the Annual Outstanding Citizen of the Year award to Dr. Clyde Wilson Jr. for his distinguished service to this community."

A well-built, clean-cut young man rose to his feet and walked confidently toward the stage. Sitting at the table he had left were his father, Mr. Clyde Wilson Sr., and his mother, Emily. This was the moment for which they had waited all their lives — to see their son become all they had ever envisioned for him. As pride filled their hearts, they knew that no one in the room could understand their sense of accomplishment, satisfaction, and fulfillment.

Mr. Wilson Sr. had always dreamed of being a medical doctor. While his son was still quite young, the father had told him he would do whatever it took to see the son become the doctor the father had never been. Young Clyde's parents had labored at many jobs over the years and had lived without the conveniences of life just to make it possible for their son to attend medical school and to complete his internship. This evening made those sacrifices worthwhile, as Clyde Jr. now brought honor and respect to the family.

As Dr. Wilson stood on stage holding the plaque, the crowd rose to their feet. Cameras flashed and shouts of adulation filled the room. Then, as the applause subsided, silence filled the room. Everyone waited for the response of the good doctor. For a moment, he stood erect, poised to speak. Then his composure broke, and with tears flooding his eyes, the young doctor pleaded with his parents in a loud voice that mirrored the despair in his eyes, "Please, Mom and Dad, forgive me. I am sorry, but I can't go on."

Bewildered and embarrassed by the moment, the chairman helped the doctor off the stage. The crowd stood in questioning shock. What could possibly be stealing this great moment from this successful individual?

As Clyde and his parents drove home that evening, Clyde attempted to explain to his perplexed parents the cause of his behavior. As his words spilled over one another, he tried to describe the frustration that had built within him over the past ten years. "Everything I have accomplished and achieved during these years has been done to please you, Dad, and to fulfill your lifelong dreams. I have become what you wanted me to be, but I have never become who I am," he said. "In spite of all the cars, homes, and other material things I now have, my life is empty. I never wanted to be a doctor like you did, Dad. In truth, I hate being a doctor. I always wanted to be a musician, but you and Mom would not allow me to follow that dream.

"Please understand. I love and respect you deeply. I know all you have sacrificed to provide me with my education, and I thank you for it. But tonight, I realized that I cannot continue living to fulfill your dreams and expectations. I must start fulfilling my own. When I accepted that award tonight, I felt like a hypocrite. Someone I don't even know earned that award, because I don't know myself. I want to live. I want to come alive. I want to be what I was born to be. *Please set me free and let me live.*"

There are millions of Clyde Wilson Jrs., and those in the making, in our world. Their lives are aimless. Day after day, they are searching for their true selves. Perhaps you are placing certain expectations on your teenager that have everything to do with *your* dreams, but nothing to do with what God has called *them* to be. We try to keep our children busy, active, dedicated, and faithful, and as a result, they may be accepted, respected, and admired, but are we also teaching them to seek the Lord in all their ways? Whether black, brown, yellow, red, or white, our young people are designed by God to have a meaningful, fulfilling life. We must do all we can to help this generation discover their personal purpose and pursue it relentlessly.

success without fulfillment

Like adults, teenagers want to be successful. The goal of material achievement is drilled into them at an early age. Parents urge their children to work hard so they can be "somebody." Schools add to the pressure by offering rewards for outstanding performances. Bookstores are filled with teen magazines that instruct readers how to follow the world's anti-Christian standards to meet their unobtainable criteria.

This relentless pursuit of success by adults has produced some unglamorous results. Divorce and suicide rates continue to climb, violence plagues every community, and mental health diseases are becoming prevalent. This is the example we are setting for our youth.

Children learn to see academic, professional, and financial achievements as good, and failures of any kind as bad. Success, in their eyes, is assumed to be personal success, deeming acclaim from others to be the ultimate approval. In many cases, the acclaim of others has nothing to do with their personal assessment and they miss the meaning of true value. If they don't allow the Lord to fulfill His purpose in their lives, they become filled with disillusionment and despair, because they allow the mandates of society to dictate their lives. Fulfilling God's purpose must be the primary goal of every teenager. Without a commitment to that purpose, there can be no lasting success.

what is purpose?

Everything in life has a purpose. Everyone on this planet was born with and for a purpose. Therefore, it is essential that teenagers understand and discover their purpose in life so they can experience an effective, full, and rewarding life — a life governed by God, rather than by society.

Purpose is the original intent in the mind of the creator that motivated him to create a particular item. It is the *why* that explains the reason for existence. Before any product is made, there is a purpose established in the mind of the manufacturer that gives conception to the *idea* that becomes the substance for the design and production of the product. Thus, purpose precedes production.

Every product is produced by purpose for a purpose. It exists for its original purpose and thus can find its true fulfillment only in performing the purpose for which it was created. Until man's purpose is discovered, his existence has no meaning.

The production of a product does not begin until the purpose for the product has been established, and the success of the project is not determined until the product does exactly what its purpose requires. Thus, all things begin and end with purpose.

This principle pervades all creation. The Master Manufacturer of all created things has made His creations for a definite purpose. Our teenagers are products of His purposeful creating.

your purpose is an integral part of you

God created you with a definite purpose in mind. Your existence is evidence that this generation needs something your life contains. Consummating that purpose does not just happen as a by-product of life. You are responsible for the fulfillment of your purpose, so the world may benefit from your contribution.

As young people discover who they are, they will learn that their purpose, identity, uniqueness, and potential are interdependent. They cannot know their true selves until they discover their purpose. Knowing their purpose reveals the particular components God built into them to enable them to achieve all He has prepared for them.

Concern for doing the right thing, rather than a desire to do things right, must always guide them. That right thing is the purpose for which God created them and gave them breath. Look into their eyes and tell them, "You are special and unique. God made you from an original mold, then threw it away when you were completed."

the principles of purpose

Have you ever watched the ocean? The constant ebb and flow of the waves reveal the order with which God created the world. With care and precision, He established basic laws and principles that would fulfill His plans and purposes for all creation.

Principles govern and reveal the normal operation or behavior of something. They are like lighthouses. They are laws that cannot be broken. We can only break ourselves against them. Just as the Law or Principle of Universal Gravitation both governs and exhibits the attraction between the earth and the moon, so the *principles* of purpose both rule and make known the *function* of purpose. There are seven basic principles that characterize purpose as God designed it.

principle #1 — god is a god of purpose

God is the source of purpose. Nature is filled with evidence that He determines the purpose for a thing before He creates it. Before the creative act ever takes place, God has in His mind the why and the how of what He decides to make. Long before God became the Creator, He was planning and designing this young generation. He does everything with and for a purpose.

principle #2 — everything in life has a purpose

If God is a God of purpose and He created everything, then everything in life has a purpose. When I look at a roach before I kill it or a rat caught in a trap, I wonder that God has a plan and a purpose for each of these creatures. God took as much time putting together spiders and ants as He did creating butterflies and flowers. It's the same with people. Just because we don't understand a rebellious teenager's purpose doesn't mean they are purposeless. Our fear or disgust do not negate their reasons for existence, because everything serves a purpose.

This is the principle we need to instill in our young people. For too long, we have let the world dictate their purpose. We, as Christians, must let them know they exist today with a distinct purpose in the mind of God to serve a greater purpose.

myles munroe

For too long, we have let the world dictate their purpose. We, as Christians, must let them know they exist today with a distinct purpose in the mind of God to serve a greater purpose.

principle #3 — not every purpose is known

Our world is plagued by the desire to have *more*. But having something is not really the most important thing. Knowing the reason for what you have is much more important. There are times, however, when the why is not known. This doesn't mean that the thing, event, or person doesn't have a purpose; its purpose just isn't known. The story of Jonah shows what can happen when purpose is unknown.

Jonah didn't want to obey God's command. When God told him to go to Nineveh and preach against their wickedness, Jonah disobeyed. He tried to run away from God by boarding a ship that was sailing in the opposite direction. While they were at sea, a violent storm nearly broke the ship apart. The terrified sailors cried for help and threw the cargo overboard to lessen the danger. Meanwhile, Jonah was sleeping in the hold of the ship.

When the captain found him, he awakened Jonah and told him to pray to his God. The storm continued to rage until the sailors finally drew lots to see who was to blame for the danger. The lot fell on Jonah, who then responded, **I am a Hebrew and I worship the Lord, the God of heaven, who made the sea and the land** (Jonah 1:9 NIV). He told them to throw him into the sea. Because the sailors were reluctant to follow Jonah's suggestion, they tried to row to shore. But the storm became worse. Finally, they threw Jonah overboard and the sea became calm.

The sailors' problem was not the storm, but the unknown purpose of the storm. Had they known earlier that the storm was God's means of talking to Jonah, they wouldn't have wasted so much time trying to save themselves. Their lack of knowledge didn't cancel the storm's purpose. It just meant they didn't have the same information Jonah had. They didn't know the storm's purpose. Unknown purpose always wastes time and gives the possibility of danger.

principle #4 — when purpose is not known, abuse is inevitable

One day, I was washing my car with an old bath towel when my daughter came to me and asked, "Dad, what are you doing?" "I'm washing the car," I said, to which she replied, "No, you're using the towel that's to bathe with." Because she obviously was right, I had to come up with something smart as a response. So, I said, "Yes, this towel is designed to bathe with, but we've bathed with it enough. Now it's time for the car to get bathed with it."

Although my daughter accepted my explanation, her concept was good. I was abusing the towel by not using it for its intended purpose. Abuse occurs when we don't use something according to its creator's intentions.

If you don't know the purpose for something, or you choose to ignore that purpose, you can't do anything other than abuse it. No matter how good your intentions may be, they are canceled by your ignorance. You may be sincere and committed toward your husband, your child, or your boss, but your sincerity and commitment cannot make up for your lack of knowledge of their purpose. Abuse remains inevitable, and you put them in danger.

The word *abuse* means "abnormal use." If you don't know the proper use for something, you will use it in an erratic and disorderly manner. Knowing this, you may ask, "How am I abusing young people just because I don't know or understand their purpose?" I answer you with these questions: Are you *trying* to see them as Jesus sees them? Are you looking past their outward eccentricities to their crying and searching heart? Are you living the Gospel as it should be lived and being an example of Christ?

principle #5 — if you want to know the purpose of a thing, never ask the thing

Have you ever asked a microphone, a chair, or a plant why they exist? Of course not, because they can't possibly tell you what you want to know. The same is true of all things. A created thing can never know what was in the mind of the creator when he planned and built it.

As ridiculous as the thought of asking a piano or a stereo why it exists may be, we have been doing that to each other for years. "Hey, what's happening? Why are you here?" Although your friend may respond to your question, it's probably not the right answer, because you asked them the wrong question.

Young people will never find their purpose as long as they ask themselves who they are, because a person or thing apart from its creator cannot know its purpose. They may even come up with a purpose that isn't God's purpose and mistakenly think they are on the right track.

principle #6 — purpose is only found in the mind of the creator

I was in an Oriental antique store one day filled with beautiful furniture and trinkets. As I walked into the store, I picked up four or five bowls of different sizes and shapes. I thought, *These would be nice dishes to eat from.* So I took them to the attendant and asked, "How much are these bowls?"

The attendant, who was Korean, replied adamantly, "These aren't bowls."

"Oh, I'm sorry," I said. "What are they?"

"These are ceremonial dishes for Korean wedding," he replied.

"Excuse me," I said, and replaced the dishes. Then I picked up some sort of thing that flapped and made noise that sounded like music to me and said, "This is a good musical instrument. How much is it?"

Again, the attendant replied, "That's not a musical instrument. It is used for incense when you go to the temple."

Again, I replied, "Excuse me," and continued my search. After I had missed four or five times, I asked him to go with me as I walked through the shop. As we looked at the many interesting items on display, I constantly asked him, "What's this?" "What's that?" "How is this used?" The attendant, who had grown up in Korea, knew the purpose for everything I asked about, because he was part of the culture. He did not need to guess at the purpose of each item like I had done, because he knew from experience how each piece was to be used.

Had I simply bought the objects I liked without asking what they were and how they were to be used, I would have ruined some beautiful pieces. Since I didn't know their purpose, abuse was inevitable, no matter how sincere I was. My friends and my family would have misused them as well, because they wouldn't have been any more knowledgeable concerning the purpose of the item than I was. Just because we all would have used them the same way wouldn't have made our use right. In ignorance, we all would have abused them.

The same principle is true for our young people. If we want to really help them know their purpose, we must point them the way to their Creator. When they discover their Creator and submit to His knowledge, they'll understand their purpose, because only God knows the purpose for their life.

principle #7 — purpose is the key to fulfillment

Manufacturers always want the consumer to be satisfied with their product. Labels and instruction books are their way of telling you what they had in mind when they created the product, so you can compare that to your expectations when you bought it. If the purpose of the manufacturer and the expectations of the purchaser don't match, the product can't possibly satisfy both the consumer's desires and the manufacturer's objectives.

Since we aren't born with instruction labels attached, it is vital we find our purpose while we are yet young. As mature Christians, it is our responsibility to help our young people find their purpose, thus giving them the key to fulfillment. Their purpose tells them what they are supposed to do and why. It reveals the reasons behind life's experiences and demands, and supplies a vision for the future. Apart from purpose, their lives will seem fatalistic and haphazard, and the events of life will become more important than the reasons behind them.

True fulfillment and peace are found in executing the purpose for which an individual was born. Just like a trumpet's purpose is fulfilled when it is blown, a piano when it is skillfully played, a car when it is safely driven, and a seed when it becomes a tree, even so their fulfillment is dependent on them discovering and fulfilling their purpose. God wants us to know His plans and purposes for our lives, because He knows that apart from them we cannot know hope, peace, and joy. (See Jeremiah 29:11.)

refusing the norm

The greatest threat to being all you can be is satisfaction with who you are. What you could do is always endangered by what you have done. There are millions of individuals who have buried their latent talents, gifts, and abilities in the cemetery of their last accomplishment. They have settled for less than their best. It seems like society is designed to make "the norm" comfortable and "the averages" respectable. What a tragedy! An even greater tragedy is that this is the legacy we are leaving to our children.

Individuals who impacted past generations and affected the world most dramatically were individuals who, because of a circumstance or a decision, challenged the tide of convention, stretched the boundaries of tradition, and violated the expectations of the norm. Few great things have ever been done within the confines of the accepted norm.

History is always made by individuals who dare to challenge and exceed the accepted norm. Why follow a path when you can make a trail? It is incumbent upon each of us to ask ourselves the following questions: Have we become all we are capable of? Have we extended ourselves to the maximum? Have we used our gifts, talents, and abilities to their limit?

I am convinced that our Creator never intended for us to be normal or to get lost in the crowd of "the norm." This is evidenced by the fact that no two individuals are exactly alike — their fingerprints, genetic code, and chromosome combinations are all distinct and unique. God created all people to be originals, but we continue to become copies of others. Too often, young people are so preoccupied with trying to fit in that they never stand out. The reasoning behind the often unusual and extreme style of clothing many teenagers adopt is not to be different, but to be like others within their accepted group.

They were designed to be distinctive, special, irreplaceable, and unique. Help them refuse to be *normal!* Teach them to go beyond average! They strive to be accepted, rather than strive to be themselves, thus accepting the minimum. It is our responsibility to help them pursue their maximum to the glory of their Creator. When they make the quality decision to maximize every fiber of their lives by fully using their gifts, talents, abilities, and capabilities for God, they will experience *maximum living.*

releasing potential

Living to the maximum challenges us all, because much of our environment is not conducive to this pursuit. In every society, there are traditions, norms, social expectations, customs, and value systems that impact the natural gifts, talents, capabilities, and potential of its members. This process starts even from the beginning of life. Even a newborn infant receives subtle messages of community expectations from parents, siblings, and other family members that, in many cases, stifle and limit the child's awesome potential.

Potential screams for release in the soul of every teenager. Each one is a living treasure chest. They arrive like a brand-new product from a manufacturer, equipped to perform and fulfill all the demands placed on them by the Creator. This is the reason why the natural instinct to dream is so pervasive in children. Encourage them in their dreams.

This preoccupation with ideas and imagination in youth is evidence that we are created with the capacity and ability to conceive visions and aspirations that extend beyond our present reality. Perhaps it is this inherent ability to explore the impossible for the possibilities that Jesus Christ, the most maximized man who ever lived, referred to when He stated, **unless you change and become like little children, you will never enter the kingdom of heaven** (Matthew 18:3 NIV). This communicates the heart and desire of God our Creator that the ability to dream big and dare to attempt the seemingly impossible would be restored in all men and maintained throughout their lifetime.

Most of our social and cultural environment works against our dreams and minimizes the magnitude and scope of the vision in our hearts. We often fear our dreams and doubt our destiny. We are discouraged into believing that our passion for greatness is abnormal and our aspirations are suspect. The result is that the majority of the earth's population lives under the debilitating power of *fear.*

ruled by fear

Fear is the source of 90 percent of the lack of progress and personal development in the lives of millions of gifted, talented, and resourceful individuals. Many experts in the field of human behavior have stated that the fear of failure and the fear of success are the two most powerful and most prevalent fears experienced by the human family. Can you imagine what this world would be like if we could abolish these two fears?

Fear of man will prove to be a snare (trap of restriction)**, but whoever trusts in the Lord** (in the assessment of his Creator) **is kept safe.**

Proverbs 29:25 NIV (author's notes)

It is reported that the newspaper counselor, Ann Landers, receives an average of 10,000 letters each month. Nearly all these letters are from people who are burdened with problems. When Miss Landers was asked if one type of problem is preeminent in these letters, she replied that fear is the one problem above all others. People fear losing their health and their loved ones. Many potentially great men and women are afraid of life itself. They never attempt their dreams, because they fear failure. Others fail to strive for their aspirations, because they fear success and the responsibility that comes with it. Therefore, the potential that is trapped within many human treasure houses is suffocated, buried, and lost to the world. Most people live at minimum performance, willing to do only what is necessary to survive. They live to get by, not to get ahead. What a sad and depressing way to live.

Challenge the young people around you to step away from the crowd of those who maintain, and join the few who are committed to attaining their full potential by endeavoring to maximize their abilities. They have a divine, unique, and precious treasure that needs to be shared with the world.

A few years ago, I was invited to the beautiful nation of Brazil to address a leadership conference. During my stay there, my host took me to visit a little town made famous by a sculptor who had lost both hands to the disease of leprosy. As a young man stricken with this horrible disease, he would sit for many hours and watch his father work in his wood carving shop. One day, the young man decided to train himself to carve and sculpt wood with his feet and the parts of his arms he had not lost to the leprosy.

The resilient spirit of this young man released his untapped potential and his work gave evidence that trapped within him was one of the greatest artists the world has ever known. I stood in amazement and disbelief as I viewed some of his magnificent works of wood, installed in the most beautiful churches in that city. We also visited his rendition of the major Old Testament prophets — twelve life-sized carvings that are displayed as one of Brazil's most admired national treasures.

Tears filled my eyes as I was told the story of this great handless sculptor. I could not but think of the millions of people who have both hands, arms, and feet in perfect working condition, but who fail to leave anything to their generation. This sculptor is evidence that buried within each young person is potential that can be maximized if they are willing to go beyond their fears, to overcome the norms and opinions of society, and to defy the naysayers.

Jesus Christ, the specimen of humanity who best demonstrated the unlimited nature of the potential in mankind, said, **Everything is possible for him who believes** (Mark 9:23 NIV). What a daring statement! It makes us question our own limitations and disagree with our fears.

This principle can be applied to all God's created beings. Each young person was created because there is something God wants done that demands their presence on this planet. They were created with the inherent abilities, talents, gifts, and inclinations to fulfill this purpose. They also possess the responsibility for this awesome treasure buried within, which can be fully released only if they are willing to believe and accept God's vision for their life. If they will learn to submit to His will and purpose for their destiny, nothing will be impossible for them.

I believe it is our Creator's will and desire that young people decide to commit and dedicate themselves to achieve the full maximization of their potential. Once again, the questions are echoed: Have we encouraged them to fully utilize their abilities, talents, and gifts? Have we allowed them to settle for the norm? Have we allowed society to

Each young person was created because there is something God wants done that demands their presence on this planet. They were created with the inherent abilities, talents, gifts, and inclinations to fulfill this purpose.

place limitations on their potential, or have we allowed them to create self-imposed limitations? Your answers to these questions are related to your contribution to the human family and to the pleasure of your Creator.

This generation has been endowed by their Creator with immeasurable treasures of ability specifically designed and tailored to accomplish everything their God-given purpose demands. However, the releasing of their potential is not up to God, but them. They determine the measure of their own success — success that is established by the Creator's assignment for their life. Our responsibility is to show them *how* to release their God-given potential.

I can illustrate this with a personal experience. A few years ago, I purchased a name-brand video player/recorder for my family. As I arrived home with my purchase, I eagerly anticipated the process of installing this wonder of technology. My children joined me as I sat on the floor of our living room to open this new treasure for our home. I ripped open the carton and dislodged the machine from its Styrofoam packing, ignoring the manual booklet that fell to the floor beside me. Then, using the basic knowledge I had obtained from others whom I had observed installing similar machines, I proceeded to show my skill and wisdom. After connecting a few wires and turning a few switches, I was ready to test my expertise. I took a videocassette, placed it in the machine, turned on the television, and bingo — play. I felt a sense of pride and personal accomplishment. Turning to my son and daughter, I said, "There it is. We're in business."

We sat and watched for awhile, then the inquisitive nature of my son began to work. He drew closer to the video machine, pointed to the row of twelve buttons, and asked, "What are they for, Dad?" In my attempt to show my fatherly wisdom and knowledge, I leaned forward and examined the buttons. I quickly realized that I was unable to explain any of the functions indicated by the buttons except those of pause, rewind, stop, and play, and my ignorance was exposed.

I learned a major lesson that day. Since I had ignored the manufacturer's manual and refused to read and follow the instructions contained therein, I was unable to utilize, maximize, and fully appreciate the full potential of the product. I was settling for less than full capacity. The performance of the product was restricted by the limitation my ignorance had placed on its functions. This limitation of performance can also be extended to those who read the manufacturer's manual, but refuse to use the functions inherent in the construction of the product. Therefore, they never experience the full potential of the machine. They only desire to experience the minimum.

In reality, this experience perfectly describes the lives of most of the nearly six billion people on planet earth. Many live on only four functions: play, stop, pause, and rewind. Day after day, they go to jobs they hate, stop to rest in homes they despise, pause long enough to vent their frustration, and then play the games people play pretending to be happy.

What a tragedy! They never experience the joy of the other functions of their lives, such as developing and refining their skills, fulfilling their God-given destiny, capturing their purpose for life, expanding their knowledge base, and exploring the limits of their gifts, talents, and abilities. They have chosen to resign themselves to settle for average. Let us not be guilty of raising this next generation to settle for average and never reaching their maximum potential.

why maximize?

It was four o'clock on a cold, wet, winter morning. The snow had turned to mush, the wind blew with a vengeance, and the entire day seemed destined to be a source of depression. The small town appeared to be drugged as farmers, storekeepers, and street-sweepers dragged themselves to their places of business. Suddenly, a young boy about twelve years of age appeared on the cobblestone sidewalk, skipping along as he clutched an old cello case. The smile and quick stride revealed his anxiety and anticipation of reaching his intended destination.

The little boy's name was Pablo Casals. His interest in and commitment to music at such an early age inspired even his teacher and proved to be the seed of destiny for one of the world's greatest cellists. Through the years, his accomplishments have been testimonies of greatness. Millions have enjoyed his live performances and history will always hold a place for his ineffable work.

Yet, after a lifetime of distinguished achievements, Pablo Casals, at age eighty-five, continued to rise early and spend most of the day practicing his cello. When he was asked why he continued to practice five hours a day, Casals replied, "Because I think I'm getting better." This is the message we should be getting across to and living before this generation.

Great minds and souls, knowing always that what they have done must never be confused with what they can yet do, never settle for great work. Individuals throughout history who have left their footprints in the sands of destiny were driven by a passion greater than the desire for personal comfort.

What does it mean to maximize? What is the maximum? The word *maximum* may be defined as "supreme, greatest, highest, and ultimate." It is synonymous with such concepts as pinnacle, preeminence, culmination, apex, peak, and summit. It implies the highest degree possible. Just a brief look at these concepts immediately convicts us of the many opportunities to reach our youth we have abused and forfeited, because we failed or refused to give our all.

This failure to do our best, to go beyond the expectations of others, to extend ourselves to the limit of our abilities, and to satisfy our own convictions is called *mediocrity*. Mediocrity is living below our known, true potential, accepting the norm, and doing what we can get by with, and it benefits no one. Therefore, to *maximize* is to express, expose, and experience all the hidden, God-given abilities, talents, and gifts through God's vision breathed in our souls to fulfill His purpose for our lives on earth. Anything less than maximum is mediocrity. Mediocrity is so common and pervasive that those who are labeled as genius or exceptional have to do only a little extra.

We were created to be above average. God never intended for success in our lives to be measured by the opinion of others or the standards set by our society. In fact, the Scriptures instruct us *not* to **conform any longer to the pattern** [standards] **of this world, but** [to] **be transformed be renewing of** [our] **mind** (Romans 12:2 NIV). It is necessary to declare independence from the world of the norm and to resist the gravity of the average in order to enjoy the new frontiers of our abilities. Why do so many of us settle for mediocrity? The answer is found in what I call the curse of comparison.

Individuals throughout history who have left their footprints in the sands of destiny were driven by a passion greater than the desire for personal comfort.

myles munroe

A few years ago, I was invited to speak at a series of seminars in Germany for a period of three months. During that time, I was able to experience the rich heritage and culture of Deutschland. Among the many wonderful memories I still carry is a lesson I learned about the principle of maximization. It occurred during my first personal experience with Germany's world-famous autobahn (expressway).

The autobahn is a network of roads without speed restrictions that crisscross Germany and many other neighboring countries. One day, as we were traveling from a city in northern Germany to the south, my host asked if I would like to experience driving without a speed limitation. Of course, I would!

At first, I was excited and anxious as I felt the adrenaline rush through my entire body. The feeling of having the responsibility for power without externally imposed limits also brought other mixed emotions, including temporary confusion. All I had learned from my past concerning speed limits — fear of violation and restrictions imposed by the law as I knew it — began to wrestle with my newly found freedom. I was trapped by the conditioning of my past and handicapped by the fear of unlimited possibilities.

As the pressure of my foot accelerated the engine, I glanced down at the speedometer and noted that it was registering eighty miles per hour. I must confess that I had previously driven over eighty miles per hour and had even flirted with ninety miles per hour on occasion. Now, here I was with an open invitation to maximize the ability of the car. As other cars raced passed me with the ease of a low flying jet, I watched as my speed gauge tilted just past eighty miles per hour. My host smiled and asked, "What are you afraid of? We're still standing still."

Not wanting to feel intimidated by this opportunity, I further depressed the pedal and felt the thrill of a car traveling at 115 miles per hour. Words cannot describe the awesome power and pride I felt controlling the speed and direction of such ability. I was beginning to feel proud of myself as we raced through the mountains and lush green foliage of the Black Forest. I was on top of the world. Who could catch me now? I had arrived. I was the king of the road, master of the highway. This feeling of supremacy was further enhanced every time I passed another vehicle. In fact, every time we passed another car, I heard myself saying, "Why don't they pull over, park, and let a real driver through?" There I was. I had achieved the ultimate. I had passed everyone else. I was the best.

Suddenly, after approximately twenty minutes of driving, a Mercedes Benz cruised past me at 150 miles per hour, seemingly coming out of nowhere. Instantly, I felt like I was standing still. My host turned to me and said with a chuckle, "So you see, you are not traveling as fast as you can, but only as fast as you will."

As his words lodged in my mind, I quickly began to understand the curse of comparison and the limitations of self-pride. From this experience, I learned three lessons that have become the foundations of my thinking concerning success and effective living. If we can adopt these principles for our own lives and impart them to our children, they will be on the road to maximum living.

1. the principle of capacity

God created you like He did everything else, with the capacity to fulfill your purpose. Therefore, your true capacity is not limited, reduced, or altered by the opinion of others or your previous experience. The key to maximizing your full potential is to discover the purpose or reason for your life and commit to its fulfillment at all cost.

> **No, we speak of God's secret wisdom, a wisdom that has been hidden and that God destined for our glory before time began...**
> **However, as it is written: "No eye has seen, no ear has heard, no mind has conceived what God has prepared for those who love him."**
> **1 Corinthians 2:7,9 NIV**

The implication in verse nine is that no human has the right or the ability to fully determine or measure the capacity of the potential you possess.

2. the principle of comparison

One of the most significant mistakes humans make is comparison — the measuring of oneself against the standards, work, or accomplishments of another. This exercise is fruitless and personally tragic, because it places our true potential at the mercy of others, giving them the right to determine and define our success.

When I was driving on the autobahn, I was in a position of great success and achievement if I compared myself to the drivers I overtook. Yet, even though I was leading all the others, I was still not operating at my car's full potential. When I compared my car's performance to all the others, I could have been considered a success, because I was leading the pack. When I compared my car's performance to its true capacity, however, I was not truly successful, because I was traveling below the maximum speed built into the car by the manufacturer.

True success is not measured by how much you have done or accomplished compared to what others have done or accomplished. *True success is what you have done compared to what you could have done.*

Consciously applying this principle to our lives can do much to free us from the immobilizing culture and environment of our society, which strives to control us through comparison. From the early years of childhood, we are compared to others around us. This comparative spirit continues on into our teen and adult years, developing into a sophisticated, dehumanizing state of competition. As a result, we spend most of our lives trying to compete with others, comparing our achievements with those of our peers, and attempting to live up to their standards of acceptance.

If we succumb to this temptation, we will be reminded that there will always be some people whom we exceed and others who outpace us. If we compete with ourselves and not with others, then it does not matter who is behind us or ahead of us.

We do not dare to classify or compare ourselves with some who commend themselves. When they measure themselves by themselves and compare themselves with themselves, they are not wise.
We, however, will not boast beyond proper limits, but will confine our boasting to the field God has assigned to us, a field that reaches even to you.

2 Corinthians 10:12,13 NIV

We must not compete with others or compare our talents with other people's abilities or potential, since we are responsible only for our potential, not theirs. Our principal goal in life should be to discover God's will and purpose for our lives and to complete our assignment with excellence.

3. the principle of experience

Experience is a product of the past and is limited to and controlled by previous exposure. At any point in our lives, we are the sum total of all the decisions we have made, the people we have met, the exposure we have had, and the facts we have learned. Every human is a walking history book. Nevertheless, we must keep in mind that our personal history is being made and recorded every day, and our past experience was once our future. Therefore, we must be careful not to allow our past to determine the quality of our future. Instead, we must use our experiences to help us make better decisions, always guarding against the possibility that it may limit our decisions. Your ability is never limited to your experience. That is why young people have the potential to do great and mighty things for God.

dissatisfaction with a fraction

One of life's great tragedies is that the majority of the world's population is composed of individuals who have accepted mediocrity, average, and the ordinary, often at a very young age. They have resolved never to be more than society has made them or do more than is expected. What a tragedy of destiny. God expects more! Why, then, do we settle for so little? Why do we abandon our dreams and deny our purpose? If we are guilty of this, how can we expect our young people to rise above our own mediocre dreams and ambitions?

Are you satisfied with your present measure of success? Have you accepted the present state of your life as the best you can do under the circumstances? This concept, "under the circumstances," imprisons and immobilizes our God-given ambition. Circumstances are simply temporary arrangements of life designed to maximize our true potential. It's not what happens to us that matters, but what we do with what happens. Much of the time we are not responsible for our circumstances, but we are always responsible for our *response* to those circumstances. We must become dissatisfied with the circumstances that restrict, limit, and stifle our potential.

Many are satisfied with simply "tolerating" this generation. You will never change anything you are willing to tolerate. Unfortunately, history gives evidence of only a few rare individuals who, driven by a passion to achieve a cherished vision in their hearts, initiated their own deliverance, rose above the tide of the norm, and impacted their generation and ours. It is time for the Church to be the ones to rise above the norm, refuse to be average, and impact this generation like never before. With our commitment, this generation can find their purpose and maximize their potential.

chapter six

As parents and leaders, it is our responsibility to teach our young people the truth. For too long, we've watered down the Gospel, candy-coated it, and begged young people to come to church. We tantalize them with a soft version of the Gospel for fear of chasing them away. From my experience in speaking to thousands of young people every weekend in America, I have found just the opposite to be true. The more we water down the Gospel, the less respect young people have for the Gospel.

Most kids don't mind us getting in their face with the truth of God's Word, as long as we don't talk down to them. They need to hear what the Bible says about God's forgiveness, mercy, and grace, but they also need to know what Jesus expects of them as young men and women of God.

What would you think about the coach who said, "Come on guys, we just want to have fun. I don't want to work you too hard, and I don't want to make you sweat too much." That coach would never win a game or gain the respect of his team. It's time for us to quit begging these kids to come to church, feeding them pizza to get them to listen, and then giving them baby food from God's Word — stuff that won't require anything from them or challenge them to change and strive for greatness in God. Feeding kids their "spinach" is teaching them things that they may not want to hear, but it is what they need to live victoriously and achieve their dreams.

ron

feeding the kids their spinach

by joyce meyer

Would anyone like dessert? Many people seem to be interested in dessert, but I have not found very many who are equally interested in spinach. Dessert tastes good, but eating desserts alone will not keep us healthy. Today, we live in a society of people who have not been taught to make the right choices. They have been allowed a great deal of gratification, and the results have been disastrous. We must teach our young people to care about "later on."

For the time being no discipline brings joy but seems grievous and painful, but afterwards it yields peaceable fruit of righteousness to those who have been trained by it — a harvest of fruit which consists in righteousness, [that is, in conformity to God's will in purpose, thought and action, resulting in right living and right standing with God].

Hebrews 12:11 AMP

We as parents, leaders, and teachers, can help young people understand that things will not always be the way they are right now — "later on" is unavoidable. It always comes. You and I can help them make the right choices by pointing out the effects of wrong choices others have made and are now experiencing bitter fruit in their lives. Likewise, we can share examples of those who, through having made the right choices, are now enjoying a great life. A life filled with the results of wise choices is the type of life to live! Wisdom promises many benefits. Among them are promotion, riches, honor, and favor. (See Proverbs 4:8, 8:18,35.)

The Amplified Bible tells us that wisdom is comprehensive insight into the ways and purposes of God. When we learn and operate in God's ways, His capital blessings fill our life.

Therefore, to one who knows the right thing to do, and does not do it, to him it is sin.

James 4:17 NASB

I like to say that wisdom is doing now what you will be satisfied with later on. Wisdom is "doing right." It is acting correctly upon the knowledge we have.

We must help young people realize they will reap what they sow. The law of sowing and reaping is like the law of gravity — it always works the same way!

For he who sows to his own flesh (lower nature, sensuality) will from the flesh reap decay and ruin and destruction; but he who sows to the Spirit will from the Spirit reap life eternal.

Galatians 6:8 AMP

resisting peer pressure

In order to maintain their individuality, young people must resist peer pressure. The sooner the better is my policy. I was recently speaking with a young lady who was experiencing pressure and disapproval from her boyfriend's mother. As a result of this pressure, she was about to make a decision to do something that really was not in her heart. She felt she had to please the boyfriend's mother to gain acceptance. I told her if she began the relationship in that manner, she would be stepping into a trap that would require her doing the same thing on an ongoing basis. We must establish boundaries in relationships.

Teenagers are very prone to letting others control them in order to gain approval and acceptance. The young lady I mentioned was actually trying to buy assurance that the boyfriend would not reject her. It may have been a subconscious thing, but the truth was that she felt she had to please the mother to keep the boyfriend.

All of us, young and old, want acceptance, but we should learn to trust God to give us favor and not try to buy friends. Anyone who is a true friend will give freedom and

In order to maintain their individuality, young people must resist peer pressure. The sooner the better is my policy.

joyce meyer

space for individuality to their friends. Controllers and manipulators are selfish, self-centered, and usually insecure. Taking a stand early and establishing boundaries helps build good solid relationships. We should teach teens to stand against peer pressure and be individuals. They will gain respect by being firm in these areas. Controllers never respect the people whom they control.

All of my children work in the ministry with my husband and me. They all made it — each survived the teen years! Each of them had situations in which they had to be willing to lose friends in order to do what they knew was right. It was hard then, but they are very glad now that they did not allow their friends to run their life. Had they made wrong decisions then, their lives could have taken a totally different direction and today they would be sorry.

The apostle Paul had to resist peer pressure.

> **Now, am I trying to win the favor of men, or of God? Do I seek to be a man-pleaser? If I were still seeking popularity with men, I should not be a bondservant of Christ, the Messiah.**
>
> **Galatians 1:10 AMP**

Paul knew that popularity with people would cost him the call of God on his life. He made right choices, and as a result, his life is still blessing the lives of millions of people today.

integrity and honesty

Integrity and honesty are not popular in the world today, but they are still popular with God. They are prerequisites to enjoying prosperity in every area of life.

I have determined to be a person of integrity, and often feel as if I am swimming upstream against the flow of what many others are doing. Sometimes it makes me weary, but I have learned that God blesses those who take a stand for doing things right and with excellence.

Integrity and honesty are not popular in the world today, but they are still popular with God. They are prerequisites to enjoying prosperity in every area of life.

joyce meyer

Young people today are surrounded by mediocrity and compromise. No wonder they often lack respect and display rebellious attitudes. Respect and honor are usually given to whom it is due, to those who live their lives in a way that is honorable and respectable.

> **Whatever may be your task, work at it heartily (from the soul), as [something done] for the Lord and not for men,**
> **Knowing (with all certainty) that it is from the Lord [and not from men] that you will receive the inheritance which is your (real) reward. [The One Whom] you are actually serving [is] the Lord Christ, the Messiah.**
>
> **Colossians 3:23,24** AMP

We must teach teens to be excellent — to do everything with excellence and to choose excellent friends. Old Testament Daniel was a man of excellence. He had an excellent spirit and the king promoted him.

> **Then this Daniel was distinguished above the presidents and the satraps, because an excellent spirit was in him, and the king thought to set him over the whole realm.**
>
> **Daniel 6:3** AMP

be an example

We cannot teach with words unless our lives back up what we say. For years, I have been praying that God would raise up and anoint leaders for our youth whom they can respect and want to be like. We must show them something — not just tell them something.

My brother had lived a sinful life for more than twenty years. He was an alcoholic, a drug addict, and a sinner in every way. He came to the end of himself and asked us to help him get his life straightened out, which we were thrilled to do.

He came to live with us. We decided not to try to talk him into being a Christian. We did share the Gospel message with him and told him to let us know when he was ready to make a decision. Within two weeks he was born again!

He shares that what influenced him most to make the decision was seeing how we lived. Watching our family together — how we cared for one another, had fun together, loved each other, and displayed good fruit — made him hungry for what he saw. I believe many teens are making wrong decisions today, because they do not have any heroes. They are lacking the presence of people with excellence, integrity, and honesty whom they can admire, and determine in their heart, "I want to be like you!"

When one of my sons was a teenager, he went through a period of confusion, because he saw "leaders" going to movies filled with bad language and even nudity. We had many intense conversations about this issue. His father and I had very strong convictions about not seeing these types of movies, but the double standard he saw confused him.

As he got older, he started making some better decisions for himself, but it was frustrating to me as a parent to be trying to teach my son to make excellent choices while other "spiritual leaders" were, by their actions, teaching him the opposite.

As leaders, we must realize that we don't have a "private" life. Everywhere we go there is someone watching us. They are anxious to see if we are for real. Let us not disappoint them. Paul dealt firmly with his fleshly passions so he would not be judged as counterfeit.

> **But [like a boxer] I buffet my body — handle it roughly, discipline it by hardships — and subdue it, for fear that after proclaiming to others the Gospel and things pertaining to it, I myself should become unfit — not stand the test and be unapproved — and rejected [as a counterfeit].**
>
> **1 Corinthians 9:27 AMP**

Paul encouraged others to follow him as he followed Christ. If we as parents and leaders live Spirit-led lives, we will be able to lead our teens into excellence, integrity, and honesty. They will live holy, righteous lives that will produce good fruit. They will make us proud of them, and will respect and honor us for giving them honorable goals.

the value of struggling

Not only do we live in an age of instant gratification, but it is also an age of ease. Worldwide, people seek to do things the easiest way possible. Initially, one might think, *Well, what is wrong with that? Why not make things as easy on ourselves as possible?*

Seeking ease has advantages and disadvantages. If we keep it balanced and follow the leading of the Holy Spirit, we will not get into trouble and will be good stewards of extra time gained by using conveniences. If we don't, we will become lazy and never develop an ability to persevere, be steadfast, and press past difficult situations.

Obviously, I don't need to scrub the kitchen floor on my hands and knees when someone has invented a mop that I can use to make my task easier. However, I have also found that using a mop all the time often leaves dirt in the corners and along the edges of the baseboard. Occasionally, we have to do a more thorough job by getting down with a scrub brush and some elbow grease.

The trouble some people get into is that they never do the more thorough job. They leave dirt in the corners and around the edges of their lives thinking no one will notice or that it really does not matter. They always take the easy route, because no one has taught them that "going the extra mile" often requires some extra effort or willingness to be uncomfortable for a little while.

Our lives are filled with "drive-through" conveniences, but I have found that we cannot have drive-through spiritual maturity. When we try to apply the same principles that the world applies to everyday living to our spiritual lives, we never grow up. We must teach our young people to be willing to suffer for awhile and to be uncomfortable if that is what is required to do the job right.

Drive-through food is very popular today, but much of it is not healthy. It is often loaded with salt, sugar, and excessive fat. It is popular because it is quick. Everyone is in a hurry and much of our society is stressed to the maximum degree. We can drive through and get our pictures developed, drive through to drop off and pick up cleaning, and drive through to pick up prescriptions. I made the comment in a conference that a person may need a prescription of medicine to help with the tension they have due to hurrying, but they are in too big of a hurry to go in the store and get it, so they drive through to get it quickly, so they can take it quickly, and hope it works quickly, so they can get on with their quick lifestyle.

I recently heard of a drive-through funeral home where people can drive through and pay their respects to the deceased friend or relative! I think if my friends were in too big of a hurry to come in, I would rather they forget it. I also saw a drive-through pawn shop in Florida. From these examples, I think we can see the direction our society has gone. Everything quick and easy is the normal way of living for most people.

This may sound like I am against progress, but I am not. Do I use modern conveniences? Yes, I most certainly do. But, I have also learned not to allow myself to take that attitude too far in my everyday life, nor to allow it to pervade my spiritual life.

I am concerned for our young people, because many of them seem to be quite lazy and unwilling to work hard for anything. If something is too hard or requires too much effort, they look for something easier, or even worse, they look for someone else to do it for them so they don't have to do it at all. Why wouldn't they be that way? That is what they are being taught by our lifestyles.

Due to our "ease" mentality, parents often want to rescue their children out of everything that is difficult for them. We have come to believe that struggle is something we should avoid at all costs, but it is leaving our younger generation without the fierce determination that is built into our character through struggle.

A baby eaglet is born with a little tooth on the end of its beak. This tooth is used to peck away at the shell of the egg while the baby is still inside waiting for its breakthrough into the world. The little eagle must hit the shell repeatedly, over and over with the tooth until finally, the shell breaks open and he struggles into freedom. The eagle is known to be a bird with fierce determination. Once an eagle takes hold of its prey, it will often die rather than let it go. I read that this fierce determination is partially built into the eaglet in the egg while it is trying to break the shell open with its little tooth.

What a tragedy it would be if someone came along and broke open the egg for the eaglet, and it remained a weak and lazy eagle all its life. It probably would not live long, because it would be killed by a stronger animal.

I read a story once that also depicted a similar example. A man who noticed a cocoon saw that the butterfly inside was struggling fiercely in its attempt to break out. The man watched for a period of time. The butterfly broke open the cocoon a little bit, but obviously had quite a lot of work still to do. Feeling sorry for the butterfly that was having to struggle and work so hard, the man decided to help. He broke open the cocoon. The butterfly fell out on the ground, and to the man's sad dismay, he saw that the butterfly was not fully developed. He watched as it struggled for life. After a short period, its struggle was over when it died. The man said it was the saddest thing he had ever done in his life and it taught him a great lesson — *struggle is what equips us to handle life.*

We absolutely must teach our teenagers and young people that the life of ease, although convenient, may not always be the best thing for their future. We must teach them to work hard and be proud of their accomplishments, and that suffering in the form of struggling is not always bad. It is necessary for growth. As parents and leaders, we must avoid rescuing them from everything that is uncomfortable. If we don't, we are contributing to their failure in life.

A group of bees were taken along on a trip into outer space to see how they would handle the weightlessness. The report came back, "They enjoyed the ride, but they died." If you provide a weightless atmosphere for teenagers to live in, they may feel good initially, but this atmosphere will not help them long-term.

Give your teenagers responsibility, make them take it, and insist on things being done right. They may not always like it initially, but "later on" they will love their lives. For example, my husband always made our older son do things right. I can remember him making the boy sweep and clean the garage sometimes three and four times until it was done right. I would often take up for my son and say, "He is not going to do the job like you would, Dave, he is only a young boy." Dave would reply, "This is how he will learn to do things right."

Today, that son is the world missions director for Life In The Word and also manages the media department. He is very valuable to the ministry. He always does the job that he is given right and he finishes it on time and without missing any details. He was born with leadership qualities in his personality, but those qualities were developed in the garage and other places like that in his formative years. He and his father struggled together, and that struggle has made our son one to be proud of.

We must be willing to struggle with our children. Some parents do not discipline their children, because it is just too much trouble. I have heard parents say things like, "Oh, just let him go. It is too much trouble to argue with him." Or, "Just give it to her. If you don't, she will be mad and pout for three days."

As parents and leaders, we cannot allow the child to take the easy way out just because it is easier for us. God tells us as His children to grow up.

Rather, let our lives lovingly express truth in all things — speaking truly, dealing truly, living truly. Enfolded in love, let us grow up in every way and in all things into Him, Who is the Head, [even] Christ, the Messiah, the Anointed One.

Ephesians 4:15 AMP

I have discovered, as I am sure you may have, that growing up hurts. It hurts not to do things the easy way. Persevering instead of giving up when things get difficult provides suffering for my flesh. Being steadfast and loyal when I would rather run away builds character.

In the same way God insists that we as His children grow up, so we must insist that our children do the same. If we provide a good example for them and are willing to nurture them in this process, I am firmly convinced they will make it.

the importance of nurturing our children

And, ye fathers, provoke not your children to wrath: but bring them up in the nurture and admonition of the Lord.

Ephesians 6:4

Nurturing is a kind word, not a harsh word. When we nurture those under our care, we take into account their individual temperaments. We don't compare them with others, because we respect their individuality. My husband and I handled our younger son differently from the way we handled our older son, because our younger son has a different temperament. Actually, we were a bit more lenient with him, but we taught him the same principles. We just used different methods to do so.

A gardener would tell us that all plants and flowers cannot be treated the same way. Some can handle direct sunlight, others need indirect light. Some require more water than others, still others can endure great temperature changes while others would die if exposed to sudden changes. I cannot keep plants alive, because I am not educated in how to treat different ones. I treat them all alike by putting them in the ground and hoping it rains enough to keep them alive. Most of them do not survive, because they need more care than that.

Our young people are the same way. We cannot treat them all alike. I am glad I have been a better parent than I was a gardener. Part of the word "nurture" means to cultivate. "Cultivate" in the *Webster's Dictionary* is defined in part as *to prepare and improve by fertilizing or plowing.* I like to think of cultivating and nurturing as meaning "to work with." We must work with people if we are to help them be all they can be.

In nurturing our children who all work in our ministry now, or in nurturing our employees, we have found that we must mix mercy with discipline. Sometimes God will fill our hearts with mercy and cause us to let something go and not deal out punishment. At other times, He will insist that we deal more harshly even when we do not want to. Whether we want to or not, we must learn to confront when God says to confront and we must learn to cover mistakes when God tells us to.

There have been times when in my flesh, I wanted to make a big deal out of something that made me angry, and God would not give me peace about doing so. At other times, I was not ready to deal with something and God would keep urging me that *now* was the time.

Part of proper nurturing is learning to move in God's timing with our corrections, not according to the timing we would pick. In my ministry, we have worked with a lot of people who, at times, I would have rather just written off. Now those people are key leaders in our ministry.

Having our children work for us was quite a challenge in the early days. We had to work through and work with a lot of things, but it has all been worth it. One of the greatest blessings of my life is the fact that all of my children are with me in the ministry. But remember, we had to work with them — nurturing and cultivating them. We had to stick with them through hard times, and they had to resist running off to something that would be easier on their emotions.

Teach young people to press through the hard times, and to follow their hearts and not their emotions. They will always be rewarded in the end.

The Bible tells us to train up our children in the way they should go, in keeping with their individual bent and personality. (See Proverbs 22:6 AMP.) We are not to train them in the way we want them to go, but the way God has ordained for them. Some parents and leaders try to make teenagers become what they wanted to be and never accomplished, or what they have become. For example, a father who is a doctor may try to make a doctor out of his son who really wants to be a singer. Raising a child this way is not in accordance with Scripture. God loans His children to us to nurture and cultivate according to His will for them, not our will.

I know there are instances when parents and leaders do everything right and the child still turns out sour. All human beings are free to make their own choices, and some seem to make consistently bad choices all their life, no matter what we do. But if we do our part correctly, the child is much more likely to be successful in life than if we do not.

What if you are dealing with teenagers who have not had correct training at home and probably never will? Is it possible for them to turn out all right? Is it possible for them to overcome their bad beginning?

Absolutely! Many key leaders in today's society are people who were abused physically, mentally, emotionally, verbally, and/or sexually. They were rejected, abandoned, ignored, and disciplined improperly, or not at all.

We need to teach them that they can overcome improper childhood training. I was abused sexually by my father for many years. Our home was very dysfunctional. There was violence, alcoholism, and abuse. The example I saw was very poor — there was no proper nurturing, the father figure was not someone I could respect, and so forth. And yet, through my personal relationship with Jesus Christ, I have grown up and done something worthwhile with my life.

Often people who have had rough beginnings have been forced to learn the principles of hard work and determination to survive. Learning these principles early in life is a benefit to them later on. What Satan meant for harm, God will work out for good when we trust Him and follow His principles for daily life. (See Romans 8:28.) We need to tell teenagers that they can overcome anything with the help of God.

love them unconditionally

People all over the world are looking for unconditional love. Loving someone unconditionally does not mean embracing their sin. It means drawing a line between the sin and the sinner. We hate their sin, but try to nurture them into wholeness through love and acceptance.

Love is the healing power that must be received in every life before we can function properly as human beings. Receiving God's love directly brings healing. It healed me and it will do the same for anyone else. Often, God uses a person to pour His love through. In my case, it was my husband, but He will use whoever is willing to lay down their life for another. Loving someone who is wounded and fearful is not always an easy experience. As leaders we must be prepared to love unconditionally. We should realize it may take some time and patience, and our efforts may not be quickly appreciated. We will be met with resistance, but it will be worth it in the end. **Love never fails** (1 Corinthians 13:8 NIV).

Kids will eat their spinach if they really believe the person feeding it to them loves them and is doing it for their good.

As leaders we must be prepared to love unconditionally. We should realize it may take some time and patience, and our efforts may not be quickly appreciated. We will be met with resistance, but it will be worth it in the end. **Love never fails** (1 Corinthians 13:8 NIV).

chapter seven

Teenagers are not a hopeless cause! Through the power of the Holy Spirit, we can touch this generation. However, reaching out to them any more than on a Sunday morning is a burden many are not willing to take on. In fact, their tough, rough, unusual exteriors frighten many adults. We don't take the time to look into their hearts and see they are searching for truth and longing for someone to show them the way.

When we present the Gospel to them and they turn us down, we quickly retreat and say, "See, I told you so. I told you they don't want any help." But it's all a facade. They do want help and they want it desperately as you will see in the following chapter. Open your heart to the ministry possibilities around you. As long as there are teens on the street, there is a need for you to reach out and touch a life.

ron

do you see what i see?
looking into the tender heart of teens
by luis palau

The story would be shocking, but I've heard too many stories to be shocked anymore. Yet, that doesn't stop my heart from breaking each time.

I met Shannon after a ladies' luncheon during our South Dakota crusade. She came to the table where I was signing books, unable to talk for her crying.

"What's wrong?" I asked her. She was a beautiful, young woman who should have had everything going for her. Though she barely looked old enough to be married, I guessed, "Your husband left you."

"I never had one," she answered.

Shannon never had a husband. She didn't have much of a father, either. But she does have two little girls. Shannon was twenty-four when I met her, but the trouble started more than ten years earlier. Shannon's father was abusive, her parents divorced when she was six, and by age thirteen, Shannon was supporting herself and her mother — as a stripper.

"I'd look around me, surrounded by people who were sick," Shannon said. "The stripping life, women dating women…and I would think, *Why am I in this life? Is this where it's going to go?* And I was always in fear for my life; always thinking that at any time I was going to die."

The owner of the strip joint got Shannon hooked on cocaine. He also gave her a baby girl. Shannon doesn't even know his last name.

When Shannon was fifteen, she was taken by two men at a Burger King and raped. "I had forty-six stitches from a machete cut," she said. "I was held for six hours straight, and I remember during that time praying, 'God help me…get me to my mother.'"

Shannon's story becomes only more incredible. By age twenty, she wasn't working as a stripper anymore. She lived in a crack house, selling herself and her baby's diapers for drug money. A man she lived with gave her a second baby girl. Then Shannon hooked up with a dealer. He got her off drugs and into the international drug trade, making runs between Colombia and the United States. That landed Shannon in prison for forty years. She now lives with her mother and two daughters.

The day I met Shannon, she had come to tell me she gave her life to Jesus Christ at the luncheon. "My past haunts me every day," she said. "The way I've lived my life haunts me really bad, and I want to ask God to help me get rid of that. Every day I feel like I'm not good enough, like I'm never going to make it. It's too much."

choices change lives

Men and women, God can use us to help prevent such tragic stories! The choices our teens make change their lives!

This generation needs to know it is possible to triumph over the world. They need to know that when it comes to making choices and when crises hit, *what* they know isn't as important as *who* they know. The important question to ask is not so much, "Am I walking in the right direction?" but rather, "Am I walking with the Director?" If they have been walking daily with the living God, drawing life from Him, the crisis step is simply the next step.

Every time we have a crusade in the United States, we also air *Night Talk with Luis Palau,* a live call-in counseling program from a local television station. Many young

They need to know that when it comes to making choices and when crises hit, *what* they know isn't as important as *who* they know. The important question to ask is not so much, "Am I walking in the right direction?" but rather, "Am I walking with the Director?"

people call in with their concerns — young people such as Lisa. Lisa's been a mom since the ninth grade. She's one of the lucky ones, because she now lives with her mom and brothers, who help her.

I think of Amy, age nineteen, who called the program because she wanted to change her life. She had her first child at sixteen, two years later gave birth to twins, and was pregnant again at the time of her call. Two different fathers were involved, neither of whom married her. As we talked, she admitted to being sexually molested at ages two and five by family friends and baby-sitters.

I think of Danielle, age seventeen, with one child already and another on the way. She told me she contracted gonorrhea from the nineteen-year-old father, who denied responsibility for everything. She lived alone and didn't know where to turn.

hurting hearts lead to wrong turns

On a spring night a couple of years ago, I received a call from fifteen-year-old Luke. Despite his few years, he had already attempted suicide many times.

"I've had problems with school, and a lot of family problems," he told me. "I tried killing myself a few times, and I can't stay at home. I have no friends. My mom is alone and I live with my dad. I don't get along with my stepmom, either. We fight all the time. My real mom and I get along, but she just wants me to stay with my dad."

Just a few days before I spoke with Luke, I received another phone call from New York. Sue, a divorcee who lived with her eleven-year-old son, described a similarly dreadful scenario.

"The other day, we were having dinner and my boy didn't come down," she said. "But since he often came in late, I didn't worry. When he didn't respond to my calls, I went up to his bedroom and was shocked at what I saw. He had wrapped a telephone cord around his neck and was trying to take his life. 'Why are you doing this?' I asked. 'All the troubles in our family would go away if I go away,' he said. 'It's better if I'm out of the way Mom, and I leave you without me.'"

That is the pit of despair, made doubly deep by being hewed out in the middle of a dysfunctional home. Thank God that our Lord knows how to lift us up out of the pit!

I waited patiently for the Lord; he turned to me and heard my cry. He lifted me out of the slimy pit, out of the mud and mire; he set my feet on a rock and gave me a firm place to stand.

Psalm 40:1,2 NIV

All of us face despair, including adults and leaders in the Church. The difference with our teens is that they're facing everything for the first time. The death of a family member, parents divorcing, a friend overdosing on drugs, temptations with a boyfriend or girlfriend, or moving to a new city and developing new friendships, just to name a few. We know the truth of Psalm 40. We've seen God on the other side of tragedy. We know from experience that God will lift us up out of the pit, but our teens haven't yet walked this road. They need friends along the way.

On Night Talk, Chris called in to talk about his brother. One night when Chris stayed home with his sister and three younger half brothers, his brother died in a car accident. Two years later, Chris was still struggling with the accident that happened when he was nineteen.

"I'm twenty-one; my brother was seventeen," he told me. "A cab driver ran a yellow light and smashed right into his car, and the steering wheel crushed his head up against the roof. Until then, we were pretty big with the church. We used to go every weekend and once during the week. My mother said, 'If your faith is strong enough, maybe a miracle will happen,' so I stayed with him in the hospital all week long while he was in a coma. I prayed every night at his bedside and nothing came of it. Now my faith is gone."

I discovered that Chris' brother loved the Lord, so I focused on the hope of eternal life that we Christians enjoy. And I sympathized with his pain. "I can understand your frustration, and I fully believe the Lord understands your anger, confusion, and desperation," I told Chris. "Even though all of us know we will die, we all think we're entitled to at least seventy years. But when the Lord allows our life to be cut short, then we have to bow our knee and say, 'God, You are King of kings. I don't understand Your ways, but Lord, You are still my God.'"

I encouraged Chris to come back to the Lord. "Let faith be reborn in you and nail your faith to the Bible, the Word of God — not to the word of men, mine, or anyone else's. Say, 'Lord, I really want to know You. I have to know You.'"

Teens are looking for answers and they'll listen to you. Sometimes the hardest, most cocky young people are the ones doing the most thinking. Don't be afraid of their questions. Listen to them. Believe it or not, they care about your answers.

Indira would have scared a lot of nice church-going people. She was one tough young woman. By her teen years, she was dressing provocatively and sleeping with married men. She called Night Talk during a crusade after reading one of my books. With every word, Indira issued a challenge. She liked sleeping with the men, she said. She loved the closeness she felt with them. I told Indira these men were taking her body, not giving her love.

Indira threw down another gauntlet. "I like to wear short skirts," she said. I matter-of-factly asked what her family thought of the way she dressed. "I don't have a family," she said, and began sobbing.

Indira's mom had thrown her and her brothers out when Indira was five. Another family adopted her, but her four adoptive brothers sexually abused her for years. Now, at twenty years old, her lifestyle was taking its toll. My book made her think she was wrong to sleep around, but was she willing to give up what comfort she could find, deceptive as it may be? How many other young women out there have never known real love, so they will take whatever they can get?

Nick is someone else who scares a lot of people. He and his friends, dressed in long black coats and dyed black hair, came to one of our crusades. Nick, nineteen years old, painted his face white, outlined his eyes in black, and wore black lipstick. Rumors spread that Satanists were attending.

On Night Talk that evening, I mentioned the Satanist. Nick called in to set the record straight. "I would be one of those people you were describing," he told me on television. "I'm far from being a Satanist."

"Where are you spiritually, Nick?" I asked.

"I've tested the waters of pretty much every faith you can imagine," he said. "I've tried Judaic faith. I've studied Hinduism, Buddhism, and Druidic faith. I grew up in a Catholic household and went to a Catholic high school."

"Nick, let's face it," I said, "if you think about it, Jesus is the only One who said, **I am the way and the truth and the life. No one comes to the Father except through me** (John 14:6 NIV). Jesus is the only One who really says, **Their sins and iniquities will I remember no more** (Hebrews 10:17). All the other religions give you a lot of good advice, but Good News is so different from good advice. Advice, they say, is cheap. But Christ comes to give us power, Nick."

Nick was searching, and he was honest. We could have debated theology long into the night. I challenged him to give his life to the Lord.

"Right now it wouldn't feel right," Nick said. "I may not subscribe to any faith really, but I follow a large portion of Christian morality." I challenged him again. He said he would consider it. "I respect you a lot," he said. "I liked listening to you tonight."

Respecting me won't get Nick into heaven. But if he's truly searching for God, God promises that He will be found. (See Jeremiah 29:13.)

listening can lead to changed lives

Eleven years ago, another young man was looking for answers, but I didn't hear Phil's story until years later.

"I remember when I was fourteen and this Luis Palau Crusade was coming up. I knew I was going to it with a youth group I was hanging out with, but I didn't really know much about it. All I knew was what would happen [at the end]. It was going to be a point of: Do you want to follow Christ or not? This is it. So I went with this idea in mind.

"I had been involved with church here and there, and my family were church-going people. Up until I was fourteen, I didn't really know what I was doing — didn't really know if I was following Christ, if the world was more fun than being a Christian, or even if this whole Christianity stuff actually made any sense. But I knew that night that if this stuff made sense and if this guy, Luis Palau, made sense about the Gospel and in what he presented, that I was going to do this thing. I was going to go for it.

"A friend and I went forward that night, and I remember myself knowing, really knowing, that this was it. Tonight was going to be a landmark in my life. I had to follow Jesus and this whole Christianity bit to the end."

Phil made his decision at our Auckland, New Zealand, crusade in 1987. I met him at one of our U. S. crusades, where he and the band he's in performed at our Youth Night. Most people know him as Phil Joel, bass player for the Newsboys. He's doing exactly what he decided to do as a teen — following Jesus to the end. And he's pointing thousands of other teens in the same direction.

Steve is another young man impacting his world. He came forward at a youth rally where I spoke. A year later, one of my team members caught up with him to see how he was doing.

"I remember that Friday night very well — January 15," he said. "I was suicidal and bitter at life and at my family. I couldn't care about anything. When Luis said to come on up, I jumped at the chance. Ever since then, I've been witnessing at my school, and a lot of people have become Christians. It's been a joy in my life. What happens is, you tell someone about Jesus and he becomes a Christian and tells someone else. Miracles happen!"

Thank God, many of our teens, like Steve, know the Lord and serve Him faithfully. They want nothing more than to walk in the ways of Jesus Christ. Teens have an opportunity unlike anyone else in life. Not only are they eager to explore life and find answers, they also have a network of people just like themselves. Those years in junior high and high school are spent at school, in sports, and at jobs with hundreds of other teens who need and want to know the truth.

Years ago, I met Nicolas. He's a grown man with a wife and children. He's a man thankful for the present, but with a heart aching to keep teens from repeating his past.

I remember a telephone call we got during a crusade in Tulsa, Oklahoma, "I just want to know, maybe you think God might be able to help me?" Nicolas asked. He was desperate to escape a gang and drug ring he was deeply involved in. He had a gun and two bullets.

We talked about common sense solutions to the mess he was in, then I asked him, "Tonight, Nicolas, are you ready to open your heart to Christ?"

"Do you think He could help me?" Nicolas asked.

"Absolutely," I said. "The Lord wants to come into your life. Christ died on the cross for you, Nicolas. He took away all the guilt and shame of the things you've done, and paid the punishment that you and I deserve. If the law caught up with you dealing drugs, they would come down hard. The law hasn't caught you, but the Lord has. Instead of nailing you, the Lord says, 'Nicolas, I love you.'"

Nicolas gave his life to the Lord. One of my team members followed up with him that night, and stayed in touch through the years. Not long ago, I received this letter from Nicolas:

"You know, Dr. Palau, the other day I was sitting down at the dinner table and my son looked at me and asked me a question I never thought would come out of my child's mouth. He asked, 'Dad, I know you're not going out with your old friends anymore or doing drugs and stuff like that, but are you happy with yourself, because sometimes I see you sad? Are you mad, because we're here?'

"At that moment, I thought back to what my life was like and what my kids and wife had gone through with me. I remembered that since the time I was my son's age, twelve years old, I had been involved in the gang life. The gang was everything to me. As I sat there looking at him I thought back to Tulsa, Oklahoma, and I told him I wasn't sad, but happy to be with them and would never want it any other way.

"What I'm trying to say is, thank you for not only showing me the way to Jesus Christ, but also showing me there are people out there who do care about guys like me. I feel like God has given me another chance in life to be the father and husband my family deserves. I guess He was always there for me, but I really didn't seek Him out.

"I know and I pray that more people like myself will make it out. If you could do me one big favor — please tell the young teenagers that you meet up with that it's not worth it to get into gangs. We have to get to them now, because it's hard to reach them when they are older. Let them know there is always a way out. Just tell them about me."

Nicolas is going to make it — not because of me or anything I said. He's going to make it because he now has the Spirit of God at work in his life. And teens, Lord willing, have a whole lot of life ahead of them.

Remember Indira? God has worked to redeem the life she was wasting. The night we talked, Indira gave her life to Jesus Christ on live television. The next night, she came to our crusade meeting. A young woman standing near her invited her to church the next Sunday. The pastor of that church quickly paired Indira with Lorena, a mature, single Christian lady, and the discipling began.

The church sent Indira to a summer Bible camp where she was strengthened in her faith. After returning from camp, she joined a group of young women in a Bible study and began to grow. Indira has been baptized and left her job, where she felt constant pressure from the young married man with whom she'd had an affair.

Indira changed the way she dressed. She changed her name. She had become a rather public case through Night Talk. Not long ago, I heard from her pastor. He said Indira is quickly becoming one of their most faithful members.

His divine power has given us everything we need for life and godliness through our knowledge of him who called us by his own glory and goodness.
Through these he has given us his very great and precious promises, so that through them you may participate in the divine nature and escape the corruption in the world caused by evil desires.

2 Peter 1:3,4 NIV

That power comes through knowledge of Jesus Christ. God does the calling. We're privileged to help share the knowledge with young and old alike. We can see the lives of young people changed and their hearts turned to the Lord.

chapter eight

Waves of revival have started again and again throughout history, because young people grabbed hold of the Gospel and took it to their generation. God has always used young people to get the job done.

Getting young people involved in missions is not an option; it's the strategy from heaven. As Jesus said, "I'm sending you out like lambs among wolves. You're lambs and you're young, but you've got youthful energy, fire, and zeal. Use it to change the world." (See Luke 10:3.)

Young people going on mission trips are not just for those who are overexcited, overcommitted, and overzealous; it should be the norm. Why is it considered normal for Mormons to send their young people to the mission field for two years after they graduate from high school, but in the body of Christ, it seems like a far-fetched idea? I hear parents pray things like, "Oh God, please don't send my kid to the mission field. I want them to be a success in life." If they aren't praying that, many are carrying that attitude.

We've got to realize that young people are our greatest asset in reaching the still unreached pockets of the world. I believe there's a day coming when it will be as normal for Christians to send their young people on the mission field as it is for Mormons to send theirs. Encourage the young people around you to get involved in missions work so they can experience firsthand the fulfilling of the Great Commission. I know God will be pleased.

ron

youth-propelled missions

how god uses youth to advance the Gospel worldwide

by david shibley

The thrilling saga of the Christian world movement is essentially a story of how God uses young people. Each day, new chapters of heroism are being written. Now, with the finish line in sight of "a church for every people and the Gospel for every person," God is once again looking for His "first choice" runners with the Gospel — young men and women with a passion for the honor of Jesus Christ among the nations.

when god wants a big job done

God calls people of every age to His service, but He always has His eye especially on youth. Throughout the Bible, when God had a big job to do, He often called on a young person.

When it was time to silence the blaspheming giant Goliath, God chose David. (See 1 Samuel 17:4-51.)

When God wanted to literally cut idolatry off at the knees, He chose Gideon (who had to be convinced by an angel that he was a "mighty man of valor"). (See Judges 6:12.)

When a nation needed prophetic wisdom, God tapped Daniel. (See Daniel 7,8.)

When it was time for God Incarnate to invade planet earth, He chose a willing young virgin named Mary. (See Luke 1:26-38.)

Yes, God often reserves the really big jobs for young people. It's not difficult to understand why. Foremost, young people often possess *gargantuan faith*. The venom of unbelief has not yet poisoned their spiritual bloodstream. Furthermore, youth have always been more willing to defy the *status quo*. Young Hudson Taylor met stiff opposition from seasoned missionaries when he courageously chose to adopt Chinese habits of dress and diet. Yet his farsighted strategy was decades ahead of his time and it allowed Taylor to identify with the culture to a degree no other missionary had enjoyed.

Also, youth *enjoy taking risks*. One key reason why God so greatly uses teenagers is that they simply don't know what the parameters are. If there is a big assignment to complete, they finish it first and find out it was "impossible" later.

Teenagers also have a great *ability to empathize*. Violence, fractured families, and jaded hopes have left today's teens all too familiar with intense pain. Since the majority of the world's population is young, this makes teenagers the natural evangelists to their peers. Perhaps the most effective youth ministry on any campus is by teenagers themselves with adult ministers serving primarily as coaches.

Young people also have *a keen sense of injustice*. When I was sixteen, the great missionary evangelist, T. L. Osborn, gave me a copy of Oswald J. Smith's missions classic, *The Passion for Souls*. I'll never forget Dr. Smith's polemic against the Western church's indifference: *Why should anyone hear the Gospel twice until everyone has heard it once?* It is this deeply felt inequity coupled with the unbridled evangelistic passion of youth that have always produced great harvests.

Finally, teenagers have *their whole life ahead of them*. The impact they make while they're young can be built upon for the rest of their lives. Furthermore, the major choices of life are usually made by the time a person is in their mid-twenties. Someone has well said that any evangelism targeting those beyond high school is more salvage than evangelism!

God has not overlooked Generation X. This precious generation, so battered and victimized by the sins of adults, is being raised up by God to seize the ripe harvest of humanity.

God has not overlooked Generation X. This precious generation, so battered and victimized by the sins of adults, is being raised up by God to seize the ripe harvest of humanity.

david shibley

leading the charge

Young people have always been in the forefront of the world missions march of the Church. In the first era of missionary advance, God sent William Carey, not yet thirty, to defy complacency and challenge the Church to reach beyond its borders. I remember standing in Nottingham, England, where Carey preached his great sermon, urging his listeners to "expect great things from God and attempt great things for God." As I read the commemorative plaque, I thanked God that a new generation of His young firebrands from many nations are even now in the wings. I want to spend the rest of my life finding them, encouraging them, and strengthening their hands.

In the second era, it was again young men and women, including Hudson Taylor, David Livingstone, and Mary Lessor, who made the difference. As the third era of missions dawned, young men such as William Cameron Townsend and Donald McGavran again changed the course of missions.

The golden chain of the Gospel's advance has always been woven by young people. Nikolaus von Zinzendorf was ten years old when he determined that his lifelong purpose would be to preach Christ to the world. Baptist pastor Charles Simeon challenged Cambridge students in the 1790's toward missions and launched a student movement that has impacted Cambridge to this present day.

Across the Atlantic, the impromptu Haystack Prayer Meeting and Williams College in 1806 launched the American mission movement. Samuel Mills, one of the students of that historic gathering, galvanized a student missions movement that reached seventy American campuses. Mills died at the age of thirty-five off the coast of Liberia on a missionary voyage, but not before he had helped form America's first missionary society and the American Bible Society.

In 1850, teenager Hudson Taylor committed his life to serve Christ and His cause in China. In 1854, Taylor sailed for China and would later found the China Inland Mission. The repercussions of Taylor's ministry continue to impact China today. In the same decade, David Livingstone preached at Cambridge, sparking another wave of missions passion there. In 1858, InterVarsity began at Cambridge, tracing its roots to Livingstone's impact on the campus.

Also in 1858, Luther Wishard suggested a summer conference for students to evangelist D. L. Moody. Wishard's sister prophesied there would be one hundred missionary volunteers from the conference. The next year, the student missions conference convened at Mount Hermon. After missionary A. T. Pierson's challenge to "the evangelization of the world in this generation," exactly one hundred students pledged their desire to become missionaries. This became the genesis of the Student Volunteer Movement that would eventually see over 20,000 American young people go as missionaries.

Once again, a missions spirit hit Cambridge when D. L. Moody preached there in 1882. Among those converted at Moody's meetings was a young cricket player named C. T. Studd. He would voluntarily give up his inherited fortune to finance his missions work and the founding of the World Evangelization Crusade (WEC).

As the fire finally began to play out in the Student Volunteer Movement, fifty-three students met in 1936 in North Carolina asking God to renew missions passion among young people. The result was a Student Foreign Missions Fellowship, which Jim Elliot would head at Wheaton College a decade later. Also resulting from this meeting, InterVarsity began triennial student mission conventions that have become the farreaching Urbana Mission Conferences, attracting some 20,000 students to each conference.

Billy Graham and Torry Johnson, a young evangelist and a young pastor, formed Youth for Christ in 1944. Soon, its impact was being felt worldwide. In. 1951, seminary student Bill Bright launched Campus Crusade for Christ.

In 1956, twenty-nine-year-old Jim Elliot and four other missionaries were martyred in an attempt to plant the Gospel among the remote Auca tribesmen of Ecuador. The cover story of their martyrdom in *Life* magazine resulted in hundreds of young people volunteering to take their place. Elliot's young widow, Elisabeth, would courageously go back and succeed in planting a living church among the Aucas.

In some respects, missions seemed to go underground in the 1960s, with the rising tides of nationalism and America's preoccupation with Vietnam and domestic unrest. Yet, God was again preparing students to launch a brand-new wave of missions expansion. Charles E. Fuller launched Fuller Seminary's School of World Mission in 1965. Oral Roberts University was dedicated with Billy Graham giving a keynote address and charging the new institution to be ever-faithful to its commitment to world evangelism. Charismatic Bible colleges also began to proliferate in the 1960s, including the farreaching Christ For The Nations Institute in Dallas, Texas.

Around the same time, Loren Cunningham envisioned youth as perhaps the greatest untapped resource for missions. He also saw that missions agencies at that time were ill-equipped to give these young people significant, short-term missions experiences. In response, he founded Youth With A Mission (YWAM), opening the way for thousands to experience missions firsthand. As one young man observed, "Loren Cunningham deregulated missions."

In the late 1960's, Dick Eastman took a group of California teenagers on a prayer retreat. A spirit of travail and intercession for their friends took hold of those young people, and as they agonized before God for the souls of their generation, He met them in a powerful way, assuring them that He would answer dramatically. Within just a few months, the Jesus Movement was sweeping thousands into the kingdom of God. Many of these young people were committed to a radical lifestyle before they came to Christ, so it was natural for them to continue to be radical — only now it was for Jesus Christ. This commitment to a radical way of life led many "Jesus People" easily into missions involvement. Many found their way to YWAM, Campus Crusade, and Teen Challenge works around the world.

Today, the numbers of youth responding to missions are far higher than ever before in history. Twenty-six weekends each year, God uses Ron Luce to turn Acquire the Fire events into huge youth missions conferences, drawing more people than the very largest missions conference in the country. Each summer, Teen Mania commissions thousands of American teenagers to go to scores of nations with the Gospel. In the providence of God, this brings us to Day One — a day to save a generation and a day to launch a generation to take God's salvation in Christ to the final unreached peoples of the world.

passing the torch

Many of us in ministry today are products of the Jesus Movement of the late sixties and early seventies, but now we are in our mid-40s and beyond. Once again, the Holy Spirit has His eye on the young. It seems much more than mere coincidence that the campus of Teen Mania sits on the very property where Keith Green and his ministry touched an earlier generation of youth for Jesus and missions. In Keith's last year of ministry, he continually pressed American young people to deal with the Great Commission. His final message was a challenge to hands-on missionary involvement. I believe it is a perfect "torch pass" orchestrated by the Holy Spirit.

What a privilege it is to pass the torch of missions passion into a new millennium! But how do we impart missions passion to today's teenagers?

First, it's important for us to *affirm them*. We should be their most ardent cheerleaders. John R. Mott believed the only hope of continually revitalizing ministries was to place youth in the highest levels of decision-making. When he was well over seventy years of age, he observed, "We must be constantly weaving into our organization the new generation. My work the world over and across the many years has shown me that young people can be trusted with great loads and great responsibilities. Youth have never disappointed me when I have put heavy burdens on them."

Secondly, we need to *stretch them*. Self-destructive philosophies are rampant, even among many Christian teens, and should not go unchallenged. Today's teenagers are used to "in your face" confrontations. Teen Mania One and Acquire the Fire weekends are major wake-up calls to a total life reorientation away from placid, self-serving, pseudo-Christianity to the radical discipleship Jesus has always required.

Thirdly, we should *inspire them*. Today's teens need to hear the story of how and why Jim Elliot never saw his thirtieth birthday. He was barely out of his teens when he penned some of the most profound spiritual musings of this century, including, "He is no fool who gives what he cannot keep to gain what he cannot lose." We need to remind our teens that Mary Slessor was changing the entire social and spiritual landscape of West Africa when she was still in her twenties. They need to know that Chinese teenagers are leading congregations of thousands, and in the last few years, almost 100,000 Indian and Korean students have committed their lives for missionary service in the 10/40 window.

Around the world, a new generation of young people is fully committed to Jesus and to world harvest. They refuse to tolerate halfhearted commitment in themselves and they cannot understand it in others. Anything less than absolute abandon to Jesus is too flaccid to impress them. As Ron Luce has said regarding today's teens, "We must show them a Christianity that will answer their cry for meaningful life. It is time to call them to give their lives away for a cause worth dying for."

Too often, we have been guilty of robbing youth of a world vision large enough to sink their teeth into for the rest of their lives. We should extend the same missionary challenge to today's youth that Francis Xavier issued to the youth of his day. He urged students to "give up their small ambitions and come eastward to preach the Gospel of Christ."

the grand prize

Some time ago, the Lord began to speak to my heart concerning today's young people. He assured my heart again that there would be another sweep of His Spirit that would usher hundreds of thousands of America's young people into the family of God. God gave me an unexpected, thrilling assignment. He spoke to my heart to invest this year back in youth ministry. The Lord has given me a mandate to pass the torch of missions passion to today's young people — the Church's leaders for the twenty-first century. In response, I'm giving a significant portion of the pivotal year of 1999 to a world tour of Bible schools, where many of the Church's future leaders are currently tucked away.

Once again, I'm ministering to youth groups, much like I did over thirty years ago as a teenage preacher. I'm finding enormous receptivity in a generation hungry for God and hungry for fathers. As I meet with thousands of young people worldwide who are called to ministry, I've discovered that God is fashioning a new breed of Christian leadership for the new millennium. The new kind of Christian leader will possess anointing without arrogance, boldness without brashness, and power without pride.

One hundred years ago, the visionary missionary statesman, John R. Mott, prophesied, "The worldwide proclamation of the Gospel awaits accomplishment by a generation which shall have the obedience, courage, and determination to attempt the task." It's my deep conviction that God is using Ron Luce and Teen Mania to help produce a generation of young people with the very obedience, courage, and determination it will demand to penetrate the final frontiers.

John Dawson has invested his life since his own teenage years in pointing young people toward the ripe harvest. He writes, "The time for big-thinking, big-hearted American leadership is not over. Brace yourself for the Joshua generation in missions, for the best is yet to come." Even in their praise and worship styles, today's young Christians are sounding out the message that they will not be denied their spiritual inheritance. A global harvest of humanity is ripening.

> **Do not be afraid, for I am with you; I will bring your children from the east and gather you from the west.**
> **I will say to the north, "Give them up!" and to the south, "Do not hold them back." Bring my sons from afar and my daughters from the ends of the earth —**
> **Everyone who is called by my name, whom I created for my glory, whom I formed and made.**
>
> **Isaiah 43:5-7 NIV**

Today's youth are sometimes referred to as the *Terminal Generation.* While some may feel this is a stigma of doom, I believe it is a prophetic declaration going back to the very root Latin word *terminus,* meaning fulfillment or completion of a season of time. I'm convinced God will give today's Christian young people the grand prize for which twenty centuries of believers have prayed, worked, and dreamed — closure on the Great Commission. That's why I am devoting much of 1999 to ministering to young people, and passing the torch of missions passion to leaders for a new millennium.

Think of it! For almost two thousand years, Christians have dreamed of fulfilling the Great Commission, and God has ordained that the young generation — this present generation — run the last lap. When I was eight years old, the gym coach picked four of us boys to run a relay race. He looked at me first and said, "David, you're not very fast, so you run first." Then he said to the others, "Billy, you're a little faster, so you run second. Jimmy, you're even faster, so you run third. And Bobby, *you're the fastest of all, so you run last.* When the baton is handed to you, don't worry about whether you're ahead or behind. Don't be distracted by anything around you; just *fix your eyes on the finish line and run toward it with all the speed you have!"* In the same way, God has kept today's Christian young people for the last lap of the race. They have the honor of being chosen for history's highest assignment.

Mordecai reminded his niece, Queen Esther, that she had been brought to the kingdom for such a time as this. (See Esther 4:14.) God had sovereignly intersected Esther's life with a one-chance, go-for-broke, win-it-all/lose-it-all situation. Even so, by sovereign grace, it has fallen on today's young generation to have within its grasp that for which other generations of Christians could only dream — closure on world evangelism.

> **But you are a chosen generation, a royal priesthood, a holy nation, a people belonging to God, that you may declare the praises of him who called you out of darkness into his wonderful light.**
>
> **1 Peter 2:9 NIV**

With more obvious intent than for any previous generation, today's Christian youth can claim this promise of God.

chapter nine

Christian men have a specific responsibility to rescue this generation. Beginning with Adam, God designed for a man to be responsible for not only his own actions, but those actions coming from his home, his city, and his nation. Many of the problems young people face today are a result of men shirking their responsibility — everything from leaving their wives to fathering children they never own up to.

This chapter explores many of the solutions for reaching this generation of teenagers. It is time for men to own up and "father" this generation.

ron

your care for others determines your greatness

by ed cole

"How many of you are fathers?" I ask the crowd of about 50,000 men. Most raise their hands.

"How many of you have sons?" Shuffling, some hands drop.

"And how many of you have daughters?" Still a sea of hands.

"Now, how many of you men are more careful about watching over your daughters and protecting them, than you are about your sons?" A ripple of laughter spreads as every hand stays up. Then I add, "It's because you don't want your daughter going out with someone like you used to be." It always brings down the house.

If we know the dangers of our world today, it is our responsibility as leaders to watch out for, protect, and disciple the young. There are two kinds of men in this world. The first are like Adam, who was created to be a son of God. When God came to Adam in the Garden of Eden as a father, He asked, "Did you do what I told you not to do?" Adam refused to accept responsibility for his actions, and as a result, lost his manhood and was banished from Eden.

Maturity does not come with age, but with the acceptance of responsibility. That's why some men are more mature at seventeen than others are at forty-seven. I said that in a church one time and a little lady sitting near the front shouted, "Sixty-seven!"

ed cole

If we know the
dangers of our world
today, it is our
responsibility as
leaders to watch out
for, protect, and
disciple the young.

Adam was irresponsible and brought sin into the world, but there came a "last Adam." His name is Jesus. When Jesus came, He not only accepted responsibility for His actions, He accepted responsibility for the actions of the entire world.

That's the difference in men. Some men cannot accept responsibility for their own actions. Others are willing to accept responsibility for themselves, their families, and the world for which Christ died. When I teach pastors, I tell them that they are not pastoring a church made up of people who gather within four walls, but they are pastoring the city in which they live. A pastor in Fiji trained his people in that understanding, and his church grew from 250 to 750 in two months! The people stopped focusing on themselves and accepted responsibility for the entire city.

> [Jesus answering the men said], **"Anyone who takes care of a little child like this is caring for me! And whoever cares for me is caring for God who sent me.**
>
> **Luke 9:47,48 TLB**

Your care for others is the measure of your greatness. Jesus is great, not only because He was born of a virgin, went about doing good, and healing the sick and afflicted, but because of His care for others. The measure of your greatness will be found in your care for others.

We live in a day when the consequences of the breakdown of the family in America are the rise of crime, abortion, teenage pregnancies, and many other ills afflicting our society. Studies have attested to the fact that the root cause of the breakdown of modern American society is fatherlessness. Fatherlessness is not merely the absence of the father from the family, but the absence of concern for the family — the refusal to be responsible for the family. The core problem of fatherlessness is childishness — immature males in men's bodies.

Seven characteristics of a child are:

- Center of its own universe.
- Demands its own way.

ed cole

Maturity does not come with age, but with the acceptance of responsibility. That's why some men are more mature at seventeen than others are at forty-seven.

- Has a temper tantrum if not catered to.
- Unreasonable.
- Insensitive to others' needs.
- Irresponsible.
- Subject only to concrete authority.

Those characteristics are the same characteristics we see in fathers whose irresponsibility is causing the breakdown of the family. Fathers must provide their children with the four things that God through Jesus Christ provides His family, the Church:

- Intimacy
- Discipline
- Love
- Value

Those four things are also what a successful youth leader must provide his group. Why are gangs proliferating in our country and around the world? It is because gangs provide four things: intimacy, discipline, love, and value. Gangs are counterfeit families. Prisons are counterfeit families. Cults are counterfeit families. When a child does not have intimacy, discipline, love, and value from a mother and father, the child will seek out a counterfeit family to provide these things.

We are the bastion, the barrier, the parapet, the one who provides to children what God says He provides His family and His children. In the New Testament, Jesus had a confrontation with people who challenged Him on his veracity.

They answered him, We be Abraham's seed....
Jesus saith unto them, If ye were Abraham's children, ye would do
the works of Abraham.

John 8:33,39

What are the works of Abraham? First, Abraham obtained righteousness by faith. (See Genesis 15:6.) He entered into a covenant relationship with God, and was circumcised as a sign of the covenant. (See Genesis 17:11.) For every covenant God makes, He gives a sign of the covenant — an external evidence of an internal work. With Noah,

ed cole

Studies have attested
to the fact that the
root cause of the
breakdown of modern
American society
is fatherlessness.
Fatherlessness is not
merely the absence of
the father from the
family, but the absence
of concern for the
family — the refusal
to be responsible
for the family.

the sign was a rainbow. (See Genesis 9:13.) With Abraham, the sign was circumcision. With you and me as born-again believers, the sign is water baptism.

The second thing Abraham did was tithe. There are only three reasons a man won't tithe: unbelief, fear, or greed. If every man in every church tithed, there would be no need for special offerings.

Thirdly, Abraham rescued Lot with 318 men trained in his own household. Today, that would translate into a pastor having 318 men born again into the kingdom of God within his own church and discipled by the pastor.

Fourthly, Abraham trained his children to follow God. God said of Abraham, **For I know him, that he will command his children and his household after him, and they shall keep the way of the Lord** (Genesis 18:19).

God's commendation of Abraham was not that he was the father of the nation, but that primarily he was a father to his family. In the New Testament, the Bible says that if you cannot pastor your family, how can you pastor a church? (See 1 Timothy 3:5.) Home is the school of first instruction.

God gave Abraham four responsibilities for his son, Isaac:

- Circumcise him.
- Find him a wife.
- Leave a legacy.
- Teach him a trade.

Moses was a friend of God who spoke face-to-face with God. But God sought to kill Moses when his wife, Zipporah, stood in the way and took a sharp stone to circumcise her son. Then she looked at Moses with disdain and said, **Surely a bloody husband art thou to me** (Exodus 4:25).

God sought to kill Moses because Moses failed to circumcise one of his sons. (See Exodus 4:24,25.) If Moses was going to do Abraham's works and abide by the covenant, he needed to circumcise his sons. But instead, he was busy with his career and left the care of his children to his wife. Zipporah was a Midianite who did not follow the ways of Israel and was opposed to circumcision. Moses indulged his son by deferring his fatherly responsibilities to his wife. God was ready to judge Moses for his failure to raise his sons in the nurture and admonition of the Lord, to see them saved and discipled.

The prophet Eli's posterity was cut off, because his sons made themselves vile and Eli did not restrain them. (See 1 Samuel 2:12-36.) He honored his sons above God by allowing them to fatten themselves on the choicest parts of the offerings of the people of Israel. (See 2 Samuel 2:29.) As a result, God took away the priestly title he had previously promised to Eli's house. Eli sacrificed his family on the altar of his ministry. His ministry meant more to him than his relationship to his family. This is another form of fatherlessness.

Eli's sons became "church-wise." The church-wise and street-wise young people today share the same characteristics:

- Hard heart
- Con parents
- Manipulate people
- Do things only to impress
- Deceptive in spirit
- Insolent in manner

The only difference between the church-wise and the street-wise is that one is religious and the other profane. Young people brought up by street-wise dads or in fatherless homes are street-wise. Young people brought up in church with no relationship with God are church-wise. *Churchianity* is growing up in church. *Christianity* is growing up in Christ.

It is our responsibility as leaders of young people to influence and instruct them not to be church-wise or street-wise, but to be God-wise. Young people may not always listen to you, but they will always imitate you. Your example is not in your words

It is our responsibility as leaders of young people to influence and instruct them not to be church-wise or street-wise, but to be God-wise.

spoken, but in your deeds done, which become a pattern followed. Training is simply teaching by example.

To train up a child properly is to set an example for them to follow. It is not the father's responsibility to make all his children's decisions for them, but to let them see him make his.

Follow my example, as I follow the example of Christ.

1 Corinthians 11:1 NIV

This is the pattern for leading the young people of today. Following the pattern set by Abraham, God wants leaders to do four things:

- Make sure the young are saved. That's our number one priority. It is what God wants above all else. God is a God of perpetuity, and wants righteous generations to follow after righteous generations.

- Leave a legacy. Men in nations are not great by the virtue of their wealth, but by the wealth of their virtue. The greatest legacy we can give a young person is the legacy of faith. We need to share our testimony of how God saved us, because when young people see us only in a Christian context, they think we are just preaching. They need to know what changed us from a sinner to a saint. They need to know that a change of heart is what changed our lives.

- Teach the young a trade. Give them a work ethic and the study habits by which they can learn.

- Give the young the moral foundation for marriage and help them find a spouse. Lower morality always leads to higher mortality. The two most important decisions a young person makes are choosing to believe in Jesus Christ and choosing a spouse.

The foundation for marriage is the understanding that marriage is a covenant relationship. Sex is the sign of the covenant of marriage. Sexual union is the consummation of the marriage in common law. We generally build our teaching about sex based on the negative: "You may get pregnant," or "You may get a disease." The truth is, the sexual covenant of marriage is positive.

Every man and woman is given a priceless gift from God. That gift can only be given one time to one person in one lifetime. When you give a person that gift, it shows they are the most unique person in the world to you, because you have given what no other person will have in all the world. Young men and women need to understand that virginity is the one gift God has given to them one time to give to one person in one lifetime.

If seducing spirits and doctrines of devils can morally eviscerate or spiritually emasculate the father, they can decimate the young people. Eli and Moses caused their sons to be fatherless. David caused Adonijah to be fatherless. They did not do the works of Abraham and disciple their sons in the ways of the Lord.

We are to ensure the salvation of our children, leave them a legacy of faith, teach them to be productive on their own, and teach them the moral standards of God's Word. They are not to be church-wise or street-wise, but to be "God-wise." We befriend them by offering intimacy, discipline, love, and value. We train them by example.

For though ye have ten thousand instructors in Christ, yet have ye not many fathers.

1 Corinthians 4:15

Leaders of young people today must decide how much responsibility they will accept. Your care for others is the measure of your greatness. How much responsibility you will accept determines how great you will become. It is good to be a teacher. It is better, and more rare, to become a father of the faith to this fatherless generation.

The greatest sight in all the world is not Niagara Falls, the pyramids, Taj Mahal, the Alps, or the Grand Canyon. The greatest sight in all the world is to see a father reading the Bible to his children. Will you be that father?

chapter ten
who are our sons and our daughters?
by ron luce

Traveling all over America, speaking to different groups of young people, and standing in front of thousands of teenagers each year, gives me the opportunity to see all kinds of different young people. One weekend, I was in a midwest city with over 10,000 young people in attendance. Between sessions, I was walking down the concourse and observing young people eating lunch with their groups. As I passed by thousands in the foyer, they all seemed to look pretty normal until I saw this one particular young lady with bright magenta hair. She was like a walking, talking, neon sign, glowing brightly in the middle of drab, teenage America.

I walked by her and continued to follow the stream of the crowd on the concourse when, all of a sudden, something stopped me. I turned around to find her (she was easy to spot), I grabbed her hand, shook it, looked her right in the eyes, and said, "Your hair looks awesome!"

She didn't know what to say. I could tell she had piercing all through her ears and as she began to talk, I noticed she had a piercing in her tongue also. She said with a bit of surprise, "It does?"

"Yes, your hair looks awesome," I repeated myself.

"Really? Do you think…" she hesitated, "well, I was looking for that place where I could sign up to go on a mission trip. Do you think God could use someone like me to go and change the world too?"

What a perfect example of teenage America — lost, confused, hurting, and screaming for identity and attention, yet inside is a deeper yearning and need to be important in the eyes of God.

I will pour out my Spirit on all people. Your sons and daughters will prophesy.

Joel 2:28 NIV

After reading these previous chapters, the question I have for you as a parent, as a father, as a mother, as a leader, and as an adult is this: Who are your sons and your daughters? Who are they? Yes, they are the people in your home, but who else are your sons and your daughters?

As we review some of the statistics of what's going on in teenage America, think about whose sons and daughters these are. According to the estimates from the U.S. Department of Health, every 26 seconds another adolescent becomes pregnant. That's an average of 2,880 a day! According to the television statistics from TV Free America, the average youth sees 200,000 violent acts and 16,000 murders of television by age 18. Of the children born to married parents, nearly half are expected to experience divorce by the age of eighteen (Larry Bumpass, "Children and Martial Disruption: A Replication and Update," *Demography 21* (1984): pp. 71-82). Compared to Children in intact families, children whose parents have divorced are much more likely to drop out of school, to engage in premarital sex, and become pregnant outside of marriage. According to the Children's Defense Fund, 2,190 children commit suicide and 5,110 children are killed by firearms every year.

Ladies and gentlemen, I present to you, your sons and your daughters of America. These are the ones we brought into the world. These are the ones society has been shaping and influencing over the years. The abuses, confusion, and bad influences are a product of the society we helped to form.

How easy it would be to think that our sons and our daughters are only the ones in our own homes. But they're not. We cannot shrug our shoulders or ignore the statistics. The fact is, it's our very peers, our adult society, who have helped to create the opportunity to make these kind of statistics and demographics possible. These are our children, our sons and daughters of America, and they're hurting. They need someone to wrap their arms around them, take responsibility, and heal their pain.

who will be the samaritan?

A man was going down from Jerusalem to Jericho, when he fell into the hands of robbers. They stripped him of his clothes, beat him and went away, leaving him half dead.

Luke 10:30 NIV

As in the parable of the Good Samaritan, this generation has been beaten, robbed, left by the roadside, bleeding, hurting, and destitute. They've been raped, exploited, and deceived by the music industry, Hollywood, and MTV. The number of broken homes in America today is astounding and we forget who pays the price — the children. Whether a divorce happens when they're a child or a teenager, they live with the scars and the gaping, wounded emotions like the ones the priests and Levites left behind on that road to Jericho. Too many of us have walked by looking at this generation in the ditch, bleeding and wounded, thinking, *What a shame it is. It's too bad so many kids are hurting, on drugs, or come from broken families.* We walk by in amazement and disgust that people could do that to their own children, but what are we doing about it?

How can drug dealers walk up to our children and offer them drugs? How can whole industries target young people to exploit them, take their money, and weaken their morals at the same time? As we go to and from our jobs, our churches, and our activities, keep in mind the fact that we have their solution.

A priest happened to be going down the same road, and when he saw the man, he passed by on the other side.
So too, a Levite, when he came to the place and saw him, passed by on the other side.
But a Samaritan, as he traveled, came where the man was; and when he saw him, he took pity on him.
He went to him and bandaged his wounds, pouring on oil and wine. Then he put the man on his own donkey, took him to an inn and took care of him.

Luke 10:31-34 NIV

Finally, a Samaritan, who's not even supposed to speak to Jews, stops to reach out to touch and bandage the wounds of a complete stranger. It wasn't his son, his daughter, his aunt, or his uncle; it wasn't even his own race. The Samaritan wasn't even supposed to speak to him, yet he's the one who reached out and did something. He didn't walk by and say, "It's not my responsibility," or "Isn't that too bad?" He decided to do something about it.

Many adults have the opinion that they can't do much of anything to really help. They think, *I'm not a youth pastor, I'm not a youth expert, I don't know how to preach, and I'm not a Billy Graham.* Well, can you put a bandage on a cut? Can you tend to a gaping wound? The Samaritan wasn't a brain surgeon, he was just someone who could put a bandage on. Can you love, can you care, and can you give? This generation doesn't need a bunch of experts who know how to preach to them as much as they need someone who knows how to heal their gaping wounds.

My brother was recently behind a car with two teenagers in it at a stop sign. They proceeded to go through the stop sign after they had stopped, and on the way through, a truck coming from the opposite direction hit the car and the car was almost instantly engulfed in flames. Not even thinking, my brother jumped out of his car, ran over to the flaming car, pried open one of the doors, and pulled one of the girls out of the car before the whole car exploded. He saved a fourteen-year-old girl's life. The next day he was on the front page of the newspaper. He had become the local hero.

In talking to him about this incident, I asked, "What were you thinking?" He told me, "I did what anyone else would have done. You just do what needs to be done when there's an emergency. You don't even have time to think — you just reach in and rescue someone." That's exactly the situation America has today. A whole generation is engulfed in flames and someone has got to reach out and pull them from the burning car. Isn't it time we take responsibility and do what needs to be done?

taking responsibility

They said to me, "Those who survived the exile and are back in the province are in great trouble and disgrace. The wall of Jerusalem is broken down, and its gates have been burned with fire."

Nehemiah 1:3 NIV

The story of Nehemiah is a story of God's desire to rebuild Jerusalem and all of Israel. Nehemiah doesn't start by saying, "This is not my problem." His heart is to rebuild the nation and he knows what needs to happen. He begins with a prayer of repentance.

Let your ear be attentive and your eyes open to hear the prayer your servant is praying before you day and night for your servants, the people of Israel. I confess the sins we Israelites, including myself and my father's house, have committed against you.

Nehemiah 1:6 NIV

Nehemiah wasn't involved in any of the idol worship or in any of the rebellion, yet in his prayer, he took responsibility for the sins of the nation. It's time for us as the mothers, the fathers, the leaders, and the adults in the Christian world to take responsibility for the sins of the nation.

It's time for us to go to God and ask Him to forgive us for not caring about these young people and not being involved in their lives. It's time for us to quit blaming MTV, the breakup of the family, and all the things the government has done to portray bad morals, and realize that this is still our nation. These are our sons and our daughters. Our prayer should be this: *Lord, we desperately want to see restoration happen in our nation and we ask You to forgive us. From this day forward, we're taking responsibility for this generation.*

a hospital for this generation

So you say you're not a preacher, a minister, or in full-time ministry — what can you do? It's time for us to quit thinking that the only people who can really do something to make a difference are paid ministers. It's time for us to look at our whole church and see that it should be a hospital for a whole generation. The hurting young people in your community should never have to look any further than you for acceptance, love, hope, or family for the rest of their lives.

Hospitals treat every kind of sickness you can imagine, and this generation has about every kind of sickness you can imagine. You don't have to be a brain surgeon to love someone, but you can make a difference. You can care for them, you can love them, you can invite them to dinner, and you can invite them to your church. You can reach out to them.

Marilyn Manson is a satanic rock and roller who prides himself that on his web page young people can invite "Marilyn Manson" into their hearts. He'll send them a Marilyn Manson birth certificate stating that they've been born again into the Marilyn Manson family. Sadly, millions of young people have already done this out of the desire for a family and the desire to belong.

Once a young person finds you, they should never have to look to a gang or to someone like Marilyn Manson to find love and acceptance. We, the body of Christ, ought to be the ones wrapping our arms around these young people, letting them know we love them and God loves them. Maybe you can't think of any young people to reach out to, but what about the teenager who bags your groceries? What about the young people who are friends of your teenagers or who live down the street? Are they being brought up in a Christian home with parents who love one another? Are they fully embraced by an older generation? It's time for us to say, "We'll be the parents and the godly, upright leaders you can look to."

If you are a parent, there are probably kids in your own church whose parents either are not Christians or are divorced. These kids need someone to look up to, someone who will reach out to them and see all that this society has stolen — the opportunity for real life from this generation. We need to be the ones to say, "Whether your youth pastor, parents, or other adults in society have let you down, we will fill in that gap. We are here to make up the difference." How long do you think it would take to reach all the young people in your community if everyone in your church saw themselves as a vital part of the hospital staff? It's not only the youth pastor's job or the pastor's job, it's also our job as Christians.

What would happen if the size of your youth group doubled or tripled every year, not because of what the youth pastor was doing, but because the people in the church were bringing young people into the church? They were reaching out to them, taking them out to lunch after church, spending time with them on weekends, and being the pied piper to love them back to Christ.

What would happen if the size of your youth group doubled or tripled every year, not because of what the youth pastor was doing, but because the people in the church were bringing young people into the church? They were reaching out to them, taking them out to lunch after church, spending time with them on weekends, and being the pied piper to love them back to Christ.

what about pastors and leaders?

For too long, pastors have subcontracted their love for teenagers out to their youth pastor. Their expression, or their desire to reach out to young people, has been expressed through the youth pastor. But pastors, it's going to take more than that if we're going to win our young people to Jesus. When you're in the middle of war, you do whatever you have to do to win the war, and right now we're in the middle of a war for this generation. The world is out to get our young people.

It's time for us as the leaders in the church to focus our attention on how we can partner with our youth pastor to really make an impact on these young people. Yes, it is the youth pastor's job to touch our teenagers' lives, but it's our job to work with the youth pastor and feed their vision. Their job is not to just take care of the kids in the church any more than the pastor's job is to take care of the people in the church. That's part of it, but we have to look beyond our four walls. There is a dying world out there and it's our responsibility to take the message of the Gospel to them. If our youth pastors are aggressively reaching out to the young people in our community, it's because they have a vision for those young people. Youth are their passion. Pastors must be a part of their youth pastor's vision!

Who are the young people in your community that your church is called to impact? No longer can you limit your outreach and say, "We're just taking care of those kids whose parents happen to go to our church." Your youth pastor should be an expression of Christ's love evangelizing this generation in your community, not just in your church. It is imperative that you are spending time with your youth pastor, finding out who the young people are who you're supposed to target, and devising a plan as to how you are going to reach them — a strategic plan that is refined and developed with your wisdom and direction as a senior pastor. Give them a commitment of resources, saying that not only are you going to have a plan, but you're going to put money behind that plan. It will take money to create an atmosphere where kids want to be. You'll need P.A. systems, video projectors, a youth room, buses, and vans — tools needed to make youth ministry viable and relatable to a young generation.

When you're in the middle of war, you do whatever you have to do to win the war, and right now we're in the middle of a war for this generation. The world is out to get our young people.

The entertainment industry, including MTV and Hollywood, invests a lot of money to reach this generation. We, as the body of Christ, must be willing to invest money into our youth ministries. People say, "Well, I don't have any money for that." We find money for whatever is important to us. We know that's true of our personal life and it's true in ministry as well. It's time for young people to take the place of priority while we find the money, raise the money, or make the money — whatever it takes to put together an effective ministry for a new generation.

What else can pastors do? Once young people are on fire for God, we need to help them see that God wants to use them while they're young. Send them on a mission trip! I believe every Christian young person in America ought to go on a mission trip sometime during their teenage years, even if they're never called to go into full-time missions. Jesus sent out seventy-two lambs in Luke 10:1-17 on short-term mission trips. He told them not to pack their bags or take much with them, because they were just going for a short time. (See Luke 10:4.)

Something deep happens in the heart of a young person when they go on a quality mission trip. That's why we take thousands of teenagers on Teen Mania trips every summer. Whether they go with Teen Mania, another youth organization, or your own church youth group, a commitment to help them go will deepen their Christian experience and help ensure that they will not be pew-sitters the rest of their lives. You'll be surprised at how many will become actively involved within your church and in reaching and touching lives of people around the world. It's a huge investment in their life, and a huge investment in their potential and their future, but it's worth it!

insuring revival in this generation

And afterward I will pour out My Spirit upon all flesh, and your sons and your daughters shall prophesy, your old men shall dream dreams, your young men shall see visions.

Joel 2:28 AMP

We look at this scripture with hope, believing that somehow, some way, God is going to pour out His Spirit and we're going to see an incredible revival happen among our young people. We all look forward to that revival during the last days.

> **Therefore also now, says the Lord, turn and keep on coming to Me with all your heart, with fasting, with weeping, and with mourning [until every hindrance is removed and the broken fellowship is restored].**
>
> **Rend your hearts and not your garments, and return to the Lord your God, for He is gracious and merciful, slow to anger, and abounding in loving-kindness, and He revokes His sentence of evil [when His conditions are met].**
>
> **Who knows but what He will turn, revoke your sentence [of evil], and leave a blessing behind Him [giving you the means with which to serve Him], even a cereal or meal offering and a drink offering for the Lord, your God?**
>
> **Joel 2:12-14 AMP**

If we do what we're supposed to do now, then God will do what He says He will do afterwards. So what is it we're supposed to do now? He's saying to people who believe in Him to quit playing the games that make you look religious. You must keep your heart clean and clear before Him. So many people become very religious, going through the motions and doing things that look spiritual, but really their hearts are very empty. In Joel, the people would tear their garments as a sign of being humble before the Lord, but they weren't very humble at all. Their hearts were getting harder and harder each day.

God is looking for pure Christianity today. You can often tell by looking into someone's eyes whether they have a real relationship with the Lord or not. With many people, the only evidence that they have a relationship with the Lord is they tell you they do. Their "relationship with the Lord" means they look the part, dress the part, act the part, and talk the part, but when you look into their eyes, do you see the miracle of a changed life, the miracle of a changed heart?

One thing this generation doesn't need is a bunch of Bible-thumping, pseudo-Christians who spout off regurgitated Christian lingo. We don't need more adults with a form of godliness, but denying the power. (See 2 Timothy 3:5.) Young people need to see adults who rip their heart open on a daily basis and cry out to God, "Yes God, I know You're real." They need to see people who, because they meet with their Father early in the morning, have a changed countenance, a changed heart, and a changed life. They are prepared to become workers in His spiritual hospital for a brokenhearted generation. When they look into your eyes, they need to see the real life of Jesus living inside of you. You ought to be the most alive person they know. Our message is not teaching them how they need to become better people. The Gospel is not a message of bad people becoming good, it's a message of *dead* people becoming *alive*.

We have a whole generation who are alive on the outside, but dead on the inside. This applies to many Christians as well, so we use a lot of Christian verbiage to try to convince them what they should do. But many times, it's just a bunch of words with no heart behind it, and young people are the fastest at detecting the phony. Why would a young person want what you have? Are you *showing* them what real life is all about, or are you just *talking* about real life? The scripture is clear — if we do what God asks us to do, to be real Christians with a real heart that's constantly opened, then He will pour out His Spirit. (See Joel 2:12-14,28.)

When he saw the crowds, he had compassion on them, because they were harassed and helpless, like sheep without a shepherd.

Matthew 9:36 NIV

When you look at this young generation, what do you see? Do you see a bunch of loud, obnoxious, wild young people? Do you see people who squeal their tires, scream really loud, and always get into trouble? Many adults in our society just put up with young people and tolerate them. Even as Christians, our tendency is to be rather complacent, "Well, after all, they're young and we just need to put up with them." I believe that's what the world does. The world sees them as a necessary evil, knowing they'll eventually grow out of their wildness and craziness. But many parents lament, "Oh no, my kids are approaching those teenage years." They have a "woe is me" mentality. We should have the same compassion Jesus had. In order for revival to take place among this generation, we have to keep the fire burning in our hearts.

Marilyn Manson, other secular musicians, and gangs have taken captive the hearts of our young people. God's looking for an adult generation of Christians who will not just tolerate young people, but love them, care for them, pray for them, cry for them, and reach out to them.

Right now is the time to sound the alarm, run the flag up the flag pole, and alert all those who say Jesus is their Lord. We've got a national crisis on our hands. We've got the biggest generation of young people coming through our ranks right now. How will we influence them? How will we impact them? It will make a huge difference if we catch them now while their heart is soft.

The world's going after them with all the fervor, passion, and resources they have. I don't want to be guilty in twenty years looking back saying, "What a sad and lost generation. If we had only known." Well, it's not twenty years later, it is now. We can make a difference. We can change the course of this generation and the course of these next hundred years if we seize this moment. We have an opportunity to reach out and capture their hearts before the world does. Moms, dads, pastors, leaders, and grandparents — your sons and your daughters need you! All the statistics and latest figures prove one thing — this young generation needs you like no other generation.

Christians, commit to act now! Then in twenty years we can look back and say, "We captured them while they were young, instead of letting the world infect them. We wrapped our arms around them and loved them. We were there for them. We were the ones they looked to as role models. We won them to Jesus, not because we tolerated them, but because we loved them, reached out to them, and offered them the truth. We didn't wait for someone else to do it, and now we are seeing the greatest revival the world has ever seen."

The harvest is plentiful but the workers are few.
Ask the Lord of the harvest, therefore, to send out workers into his harvest field.

Matthew 9:37,38 NIV

Ron Luce—*Profile*

President and CEO of **Teen Mania Ministries,** a national youth missions organization, based in Garden Valley, Texas. The following four areas envelope the purpose and mission of Teen Mania:

- **Missions:** Last year, 3,200 teenagers were sent out to 30 different countries. This year, Teen Mania is preparing to take 10,000 teenagers to 50 different countries.

- **ATF:** Ron hosts national youth conventions across North America called **"Acquire The Fire".** Thousands of teens gather each weekend for a contemporary presentation of radical Christian living including mammoth video walls, a live worship band, comic sketches, and pyrotechnics. Over 147,000 teens attended last year in 27 cities. 175,000 will be attending this year in 25 cities.

- **Dome Event:** This year Ron will host Teen Mania's first dome event to be held in Pontiac, Michigan on April 23 & 24, 1999. 80,000 are expected in attendance and it will be a millennium gathering that will serve as a battle cry for this generation. "Fathers of the faith" all over the nation are standing with us at this event, as a statement that they believe in this young generation.

- **Internship/Campus**: Our Honor Academy Program disciples and develops high school graduates and college students for an entire year producing some of the finest delegates for the workplace. There are currently 519 young people enrolled in the Honor Academy and we are expecting a total class of 730 Honor Academy participants in August. Our campus consists of 464 acres and construction has been progressing quickly, developing Teen Mania into a world class facility.

Raised in a broken home and after several years of drug and alcohol abuse, Ron ran away at the age of 15 before finding Jesus at age 16.

Bachelor of Arts in psychology and theology from Oral Roberts University.

Master of Arts in counseling and psychology from the University of Tulsa.

Hosts a weekly television program called **Acquire the Fire** for teenagers, shown on Trinity Broadcasting Network.

Authored *Inspire the Fire,* a book for parents of teenagers.

Authored *56 Days Ablaze,* a devotional for teens.

Authored *Quit Playing with Fire,* a book for teenagers on how to deal with difficult issues and for parents to know how to work with their teenagers on these issues.

Authored *10 Challenges of a World Changer,* a devotional study guide, guiding readers through ten specific challenges that the teenager will commit to meet if they are to answer that call.

Authored *Mark of a World Changer,* a devotional study guide, guiding readers to make their mark on the world by building their life with character, not hype, and by utilizing the ten challenges studied in the previous devotional study guide to build that character in themselves.

Co-authored with Carman *R.I.O.T. Manual,* a book for teenagers on how to start a R.I.O.T. — Righteous Invasion Of Truth — in their own town.

Consulting Editor for the *Promise Bible for Students,* a Bible that touches base with many issues teens face today, encouraging and challenging them with words that speak their language. (CEV)

Authored *Mature Christians Are Boring People... And Other Myths About Maturing in Christ,* a devotional book for teens that identifies wrong assumptions about maturity in Christ and how to combat negative peer pressure.

Authored *Rescue Manual for Parents,* a book for parents on how to deal with pressing teen issues.

Authored *Spiritual Shock Treatment,* his latest devotional for teens.

Worship leader for five Teen Mania worship albums the latest being *Worship Shock Treatment for the Soul.*

Guest appearances on Dr. James Dobson's "Focus on the Family" radio broadcast.

Traveled to more than 50 countries, taking the Gospel to the world.

Guest host on the 700 Club and appeared several times as a guest on Trinity Broadcasting Network.

Ron and his wife Katie have three children; Hannah, Charity, and Cameron.

Books by Ron Luce

Spiritual Shock Treatment — Get Real With Jesus (Teen Devotional)

Rescue Manual for Parents

*Mature Christians Are Boring People… And
Other Myths About Maturity in Christ*

*R.I.O.T. Manual
(co-authored with Carman)*

Inspire the Fire

56 Days Ablaze

Quit Playing with Fire

10 Challenges of a WorldChanger

Mark of a WorldChanger

To contact Ron Luce or Teen Mania Ministries, please write:

P. O. Box 2000

Garden Valley, Texas 75771-2000

Additional copies of this book and other book titles
from **ALBURY PUBLISHING** are
available at your local bookstore.

ALBURY PUBLISHING
P. O. Box 470406
Tulsa, Oklahoma 74147-0406

In Canada books are available from:
Word Alive
P. O. Box 670
Niverville, Manitoba
CANADA ROA 1E0

It's a question of vision. Not just if yours is good, but whether or not you have one for your future. And while you're examining your vision, check out your hearing too. Is God calling you to build a bedrock of Christ-like character while pouring your life out for others at the Teen Mania Honor Academy?

At Teen Mania, our vision is to mobilize a generation of young people who will minister around the world to those who have never had the chance to hear the Gospel. One thing... it takes a dedicated, disciplined team of people willing to live selfless lives for Christ to pull off such an undertaking. Are you willing to be one of them?

EXAMINE YOUR OPTIONS:

ONE-YEAR INTERNSHIP
For high school graduates who desire to develop Christian character and leadership skills while investing a year to reach the world before pursuing further education or career.

TWO-YEAR APPRENTICESHIP
For college graduates who wish to gain invaluable ministry experience and focus for their lives while working in a leadership position at Teen Mania headquarters or traveling with our various teams.

ONE-YEAR MINISTRY INTERNSHIP
An opportunity for those 21 and older to develop ministry and technical skills on the road while ministering to youth across North America by assisting with our ATF conventions.

The opportunities for leadership, career development and travel are great. The rewards will last a lifetime... and beyond. Find out more. Call 1.800.299.TEEN today.

P.O. Box 2000
Garden Valley, TX 75771-2000
www.teenmania.org

Is it ignorance?

Or willful blindness? This habit of living in one's own little world. A world where deciding what to wear or whether or not to "super size it" seems to matter.

Then something interesting happens. We answer God's call to take the blinders off. And suddenly, we see that we're part of a much bigger world. The Real World. Where children go to bed hungry. Entire villages live in poverty. And countless people have never heard of the saving love of Jesus Christ.

An adventurous, life-changing Teen Mania summer mission trip lets you see the world in this new light - while showing others the way to salvation.

Lose the blinders. Gain a new perspective. And send for your free, 32-page summer missions guide. You just might see God's light at the end of your tunnel vision.

If you want to see the world through God's eyes, just call us toll free at 1-800-299-TEEN for your free, 32-page Teen Mania summer missions guide. *Let's change the world this summer!*

LEADERSHIP OPPORTUNITIES

God is raising up a new generation to change this world. Now, more than ever before, these young people need leaders to rise up and lead them.

If you possess strong character, a disciplined relationship with God, if you have any leadership experience, you could be eligible for a leadership role on a Teen Mania mission trip this summer.

Positions available are Team Leader (21+ years old), Missionary Advisor (18-25 years old) and Country Assistant.

If any of these leadership opportunities sound like an adventure to you, just call us at our toll free number **1-800-299-TEEN** (ext. **8091**) for more information on leadership opportunities with Teen Mania.

YOUTH GROUP MISSIONS TRIPS

Are you ready to see your youth group go to the next level? Can you get a vision for stepping outside the normal youth group activities and stepping into an adventure that will yield eternal results? Come on a summer missions trip, and see your group involved in fulfilling the Great Commission!

Funding, planning, and executing such a trip may seem like an impossible task, but that's why Teen Mania is here. For years, they have handled all facets of such an excursion. From fundraising tips to travel arrange-

ments, Teen Mania's staff can guide you through it all.

Just imagine your group involved in changing the world for the glory of God! Call toll free **1-800-299-TEEN** for more information on Teen Mania's youth group trips.

Teen Mania Ministries
P.O. Box 2000
Garden Valley, TX 75771-2000
www.teenmania.org